NOW THE JOYFUL CELEBRATION

NOW THE JOYFUL CELEBRATION

Hymns, Carols, and Songs

by

Jaroslav J. Vajda

MorningStar
MUSIC PUBLISHERS

Prompt arrangements can be made for permission for a church congregation to reproduce single hymns for service use, as well as for wider use of the texts copyright by Jaroslav Vajda in this book. Such permission must be obtained in writing from the author in care of Morning Star Music Publishers at 3303 Meramec Street, St. Louis, MO 63118-4310. Phone (314) 352-3303.

Library of Congress Cataloging-in-Publication Data

Vajda, Jaroslav. J., 1919-
    Now the joyful celebration.

    Includes indexes.
        1. Lutheran Church—Hymns.   2. Hymns, English.
    I. Title
    BV410.V35   1987   264'.04102   87-24883

    ISBN: 0-944529-01-1

Book Design by Ruth Lewis
Printed in the United States of America

Copyright © 1987 Morning Star Music Publishers
3303 Meramec, Suites 205-207, St. Louis, MO 63118-4310

To my wife Louise —
constant companion, supporter and inspiration
in our struggles with worship
on the journey of faith

ACKNOWLEDGMENTS

There is no proper beginning or end to the list of persons who directly or indirectly influenced the texts in these pages. One is sure to omit an important name or event, only to remember it after the book is in print. So this can be only a temporary listing of some of the people to whom I must express gratitude.

In addition to those mentioned in the introduction, I pay this modest tribute to my wife Louise for her understanding, support, and encouragement as my gentle critic; to my parents, John and Mary Vajda, of course, for their genes, their spiritual legacy and sacrifices; to Carl Schalk, who proved that *Now the silence* could be a hymn and that he could compose melodies that would capture the mood and movement of other texts in a way that could only have been inspired; and to other composers who have made my texts accessible to the worshiping community with truly fitting settings.

Thanks are due those hymnal committees who have found a number of hymns worthy of inclusion in their hymnals (see Appendix 1 and 2); the publishers of sheet music (see Appendix 3); and Rodney Schrank and Morning Star Music Publishers for making this collection available in book form.

But primary and central to this entire project: the Holy Spirit, that most precious Gift of our glorious Savior Jesus Christ, to whose honor these texts are dedicated.

Jaroslav J. Vajda

CONTENTS

FOREWORD

It was in 1969—the year of his fiftieth birthday—that Jaroslav Vajda first came to prominent attention as a translator and writer of hymns. That year saw the publication of *Worship Supplement*, a product of the Commission on Worship of The Lutheran Church—Missouri Synod, containing four of Vajda's texts. Two were translations of texts from Vajda's Slovak heritage; two were original texts which first appeared in that volume.

Of the two original texts which appeared in *Worship Supplement*, one—"Now the silence," an Entrance hymn for the Holy Communion—quickly won the attention of a wide public. Pronounced a *tour de force* by Erik Routley, an "example of the new talent for poetry" being fostered in American hymnody, it soon found a place in a large number of hymnals in the years following its appearance. Its broad acceptance placed the name and work of Jaroslav Vajda at center stage, a writer of hymn texts to be reckoned with.

The groundwork for Vajda's interest in hymnody had been a long time in preparation. The grandson of immigrants from Slovakia, he grew up in a home where the old traditions and language were preserved. Early in his life he was introduced to the treasures of Slovak culture, especially the riches of its hymnody. Names such as Tranovský and Kuchárik and collections such as the *Cithara Sanctorum* (the "Tranoscius") and the *Duchovná Cithara* were familiar companions in the Vajda home. In his years at the seminary, he received an education which placed heavy emphasis on the study of classical languages. Such a background, together with a fluent grasp of the Slovak language first learned as a child, provided the solid basis for the development of the skills necessary to begin translating some of the literature and hymnody of Vajda's own Slovak heritage, a task he soon began. Such a background also helped foster an attitude of loving care in the use of language that would be of inestimable worth in fashioning original texts. His vocation as pastor and preacher, and later as editor and book developer, helped to hone the skills necessary to both the translator's and hymn writer's art: clarity of imagery and the ability to convey that imagery with economy and power.

Three aspects of Vajda's writing deserve special comment. First is Vajda's ability to fashion a striking new image, or to reshape an older image, recasting it in a way which brings fresh insight and understanding. To mention such lines from his carol "Before the marvel of this night" as "Then tear the sky apart with light" or "Give earth a glimpse of heavenly bliss / A teasing taste of what they miss" is simply to begin to touch the surface of writing consistently marked by fresh, sparkling turns of phrases and vibrant imagery. Similar examples occur again and again in Vajda's work.

A second important aspect of Vajda's writing is his affinity for less usual textual forms and meters, less usual at least in the context of traditional hymnody. The 103 texts in this collection, utilizing 64 different metrical patterns in addition to 19 texts set to irregular meter, are a testimony to this inclination. It is interesting to observe that the texts which are among his most successful tend to fall among those written in unusual metrical patterns. "Amid the world's bleak wilderness" (in the classic form of the *terza rima*), "Christ goes before" and "Now the silence" (both Irregular), "God of the sparrow, God of the whale" (5.4.6.7.7.), and "You are the king" (written in sonnet form), are a few examples among many which employ forms and meters not normally associated with traditional hymnody. This aspect of Vajda's style obviously presents a unique challenge to musicians who would attempt to set these texts to music intended for congregational singing. That many of these texts have been successfully set for singing by ordinary congregations is a tribute, first of all, to the stimulation and generative force of textual forms requiring new and different musical solutions.

A third aspect of Vajda's writing is the strong theological thrust of his texts. The notes to each of the texts in this volume reflect that concern, and a study of these notes will be amply repaid with insights into the workings of a mind not only creatively fertile linguistically, but biblically grounded and theologically informed as well. Trinitarian language, for example, not only informs much of Vajda's writing, it frequently determines structure as well. Such texts as "God, who built this wondrous planet," "O God, eternal Father, Lord," "Up through endless ranks of angels," "Now the silence," and "Go, my children, with my blessing" are obvious examples. Other "songs in threes" include "Before the marvel of this night," "Begin the song of glory now" and "Christ goes before."

Special mention must also be made of the significant number of texts designed for particular liturgical uses and needs. Hymns for baptism, communion, and dismissal, fresh psalm paraphrases, and Entrance, Kyrie, and Credo hymns, as well as hymns for various times of the church year form a substantial part of Vajda's writing.

Amid the current flood of hymnody—so much of it bland and insipid, on the one hand, or obtuse and overly clever, on the other—the work of Jaroslav Vajda stands as a unique testimony to clarity of expression, careful craftsmanship, and theological integrity. His writing is in the mainstream, accessible and popular in the best sense of both words. At the same time, Vajda is careful to avoid the trendiness in style, language, and subject matter which was virtually *de rigueur* in the 60s and 70s, and which still afflicts much contemporary hymnody. Vajda's hymnody is, to be sure, both the result and the expression of one man's lifelong spiritual journey, yet it is a journey which we all—in one way or another—share.

In a beautiful passage from his writing *On the Last Words of David*, Martin Luther [with parenthetical additions by this writer] wrote:

> St. Ambrose [and Jaroslav Vajda] composed many hymns of the church. They are called church hymns because the church accepted and sings them just as though the church had written them and as though they were the church's song. Therefore it is not customary to say, "Thus sings Ambrose, Gregory, Prudentius, Sedulius, [and Vajda]" but "Thus sings the Christian church." For these are now the songs of the church, which Ambrose, Sedulius, [and Vajda] etc., sing with the church and the church with them. When they die, the church survives them and keeps on singing their songs.

Ultimately, the texts of Jaroslav Vajda are a sign to God's people, a sign of hopefulness, expectation, and promise. For they are a sign that the Holy Spirit has not forsaken his church, and that we are still given new songs to sing—songs which the church will surely continue to sing along its pilgrim way until that time when all its singing will be joined to that last and greatest song of the Lamb in eternity.

Carl Schalk
River Forest, Illinois
May 29, 1987

The Commemoration of Jiři Tranovský, hymn writer, 1637

REFLECTIONS ON HYMN WRITING

Difficult as it is for me to believe that a number of my hymns appear in several major hymnals, I find it even more difficult to believe that I wrote them. That they exist at all is testimony to the grace and leading of God the giver and blesser of every gift.

This introduction to an anthology of hymns, songs, and carols I have either written or translated provides a rare opportunity to outline some of the goals and procedures followed in the preparation of these texts. I leave the literary critique of poetry and hymn writing to experts in the field. Here I shall note what only I can say with authority about my hymn writing and translating: why I write hymns and how I write them. Beyond that the texts will have to stand on their own merits as offerings to God and his people as instruments of worship.

Like others, I am fascinated by any shred of background information regarding the authorship of hymns: who the writer was, what influences molded his or her life, and under what circumstances the text was written. While laying no claims to immortality, I justify recording selected observations of my life and influences thereon as a part of my rationale for writing hymns. When I examine my life experiences as a child of God, I see how all things work together to supply background and substance to one's creative writing. From the vantage point of 67 years I discover the leading and protecting hand of God and the preparation of the Holy Spirit for my life's calling. I have had to wait until now to understand and appreciate events that seemed meaningless or unimportant when they were happening.

I suspect I write hymns for many of the same reasons others do. In my case, because I am who I am: a certain male born to certain parents in a certain place at a certain time. And then because of certain influences which have left their mark on many hymn texts. A number of autobiographical observations will appear in the background notes to the texts in this anthology. At this place and time, however, I will point out some elements I feel have contributed in some way to what has now become a third career: hymn writing and translating.

My name immediately betrays my ancestry and suggests recent

immigration. Actually, both sets of grandparents (the Vajdas and Gecys) emigrated from Slovakia (the eastern third of present-day Czechoslovakia) in the late 1880s. Both my parents were born in the vicinity of Hazleton, Pennsylvania, where Grandfather George Vajda owned a small grocery store and Grandfather Michael Gecy was a brewmaster in a local brewery. My father, John, the oldest of four children in a mixed Lutheran/Catholic family, was encouraged by Mr. Gecy to leave the coal mines and to prepare for the Lutheran ministry. He went to Concordia Theological Seminary in Springfield, Illinois, graduating in 1918, whereupon he married his hometown fiancee, Mary Gecy, a floorlady in the Hazleton silk mill and church organist.

I was born in Lorain, Ohio, my father's first pastorate, and, like Martin Luther, was given the Slavic saint's name whose day fell on April 27. That explains Jaroslav. But the ethnic heritage went deeper than the name. Acquaintance with the Slovak language from birth provided an entree into a rich culture and literature, but most importantly, to the treasures of Slavic hymnody.

My father's calling took the family from Lorain, Ohio, to Emporia, Virginia, where my brother Ludovit was born, and then to Racine, Wisconsin, where I remember the doctor coming to our parsonage to deliver Eduard, five years my junior. By 1926, when I was seven, we arrived at the steel and refinery community of Indiana Harbor (later, East Chicago), near the Indiana-Illinois state line. There my father remained until his retirement, serving a bilingual congregation.

It was in that sooty industrial town that I attended a one-room "German" Lutheran school through the elementary grades, then went on to a public high school for two years, and at the age of 13 went with a neighboring pastor's son to visit Concordia College in Fort Wayne and stayed to begin my training for the Lutheran ministry.

Along with a foreign language facility, I inherited something much more important from my parents: their nurture of my baptismal faith and positive spiritual values. I am indebted to them also for their model of dedication, their self-sacrificing support of their three sons, all of whom entered the ministry, and their provision of music lessons — all of which left an indelible mark on my character, personality, and eventually, my hymn writing.

In those pre-seminary years, two other experiences portended impressions that affected my hymn writing. One was a visit to our East Chicago parsonage by a delegation from the cultural Institute of Slovakia when I was 15. The trio, a leading novelist, an archeologist and artist, and a historian, left a box of books containing the classic literature of Slovakia. Discovering that treasure, I determined to translate some of it into English, eventually rendering some 100 poems by 40 Slovak and Czech poets in English, including a 32-sonnet sequence by Pavol Országh Hviezdoslav (1849-1921), Slovakia's greatest poet. A phrase from one of his lyrics provided me subconsciously with the opening line of *Now the silence* 15 years later.

The other impetus was provided by O. P. Kretzmann, whom my generation may remember as the outstanding literary figure in the Lutheran Church—Missouri Synod, who founded *The Cresset*, a Christian journal of literature and the arts. When I submitted several poems to *The Cresset* as an 18-year-old student, this highly respected editor wrote me a note, saying, "You have an authentic gift for poetry." I can hardly estimate the effect those seven words had on my determination to write poetry, and eventually hymns.

Other people and books and experiences combined to direct and enrich my literary efforts, not the least of which was my marriage to Louise, nee Mastaglio, of Milwaukee, with her lay background, her musical and literary talents, and her editorial criticism and demand for a practical application of Christian doctrine and integrity. Her bearing and nurture of our four children (Susan, Jeremy, Timothy, and Deborah) tested the validity of the family virtues propounded by her husband from the pulpit and familiarized me with the potentials of the family at first hand. Since one of my hymn-writing principles is to presume to write only about what I know from the Scriptures and from my own experiences, being a husband and father gives my hymns on marriage and the family an authenticity they might otherwise lack.

Further background for hymn writing comes from 18 years in the parish ministry, where worship services had to be planned and conducted, and where one soon discovered which ingredients were effective or were lacking. Add to this 16 years as a working member of two worship commissions, the Commission on Worship of The Lutheran Church—Missouri Synod which prepared the 1969

Worship Supplement, which proved to be such a rich resource for other hymnals, and the Inter-Lutheran Commission on Worship which put together the *Lutheran Book of Worship* in 1978. On both commissions we evaluated more than 2,000 hymn texts, struggled with theological and hymnic criteria, examined contemporary worship needs and were among the first commissions to contend with the issue of sexist language. It was an invaluable and enviable experience few hymn writers are given, but which they must duplicate on a smaller scale as they hammer out their own standards for self-criticism.

The past 24 years have contributed additional equipment for literary production. In 1963 I was appointed editor of *This Day*, a Christian monthly family magazine, a position that sharpened my critical skills, which were later applied to the profession of book developer/editor for Concordia Publishing House. In the course of 15 years, I saw 200 books through from concept to publication, during the course of which I had to read and evaluate hundreds of submissions on every subject even remotely related to Christianity, the church, and Christian living—clearly a procession of concerns that God's people have to deal with during their earthly pilgrimage and which somehow get into the worship life if it is to have any relevance at all to life in today's world.

It is this world and this life in it where God meets us and we him. And that world, though in basic ways like the world of the past, is for my generation drastically different from the one I knew as a child. The form of the Christian community has changed for better or for worse, but changed irrevocably. It is no use trying to import many of the traditions of the past into a generation that can no longer maintain the traditional family structure. If *This Day* were still being published, it would have to be even more concerned than it was 20 years ago with singles, stepfamilies, divorce, abortion, and other family concerns. How can today's families express their needs in hymns that come out of a pattern no longer familiar to one-half the worshipers?

So the hymn writer must speak for the generation in which he is writing. And that means adapting the expressions of the saints of old to current conditions and experiences. The Middle Ages had their plagues; we have our AIDS. The Reformers struggled with corrupt religion; we wrestle with the cults. The contemporaries of Christ fought demons dead bent on destroying their faith; we fight the enslavement of drugs, the wasters of innocence and life, the madmen with nuclear weapons at their disposal. Our ancestors could take delight and refreshment in a relatively uncorrupted nature, whereas we face the prophetic, if not too-late, task of halting the pollution of our natural resources. We live in an age of short-term values, of the trivialization of life, the risking of the future for immediate gain; growing racial prejudice and hostility, and greater reliance on arms than on God.

Although life has always been a struggle, the church today must speak to the specific concerns of the day. It cannot escape the hungry and the homeless, the oppressed and the captives while at the same time maintaining an optimism that there are divine solutions to human problems and that Christ is still the only hope the world has. The task of the church, and of hymnody, is to give voice both to the cries and to the Gospel. It is to lift the eyes of people to the hills whence our help comes, and to reaffirm that our help is in the name of the Lord.

And this speaking and singing must be done in the language of today. In the Lutheran tradition, this means restating the substance of the lengthy chorales in the imagery and idioms of today's worshipers, perhaps as I tried to do in "The rescue we were waiting for." And new poetic forms may help to make the content of worship more immediate to a generation whose attention span and literary allusions border on the minimal. We have discovered that hymns can be written without rhyme, as was demonstrated ages ago with "Adeste fideles," and as I learned when Carl Schalk proved that "Now the silence" could be set to music and serve as an Entrance hymn. Herbert Brokering's "Earth and all stars" demonstrates a similar effective use of free verse in hymnody.

All in all, hymn writing for me is one aspect of my lifelong struggle with worship. Only in retrospect did I discover that this struggle was going on from childhood as I attended church services regularly, and it continued as I moved into the position of worship planner and leader. And I found it there in full force as I began writing hymns. The catalyst of the inner debate was Psalm 122, which David begins with a statement I had often dismissed as a poetic exaggeration. Was he really glad when they said to him: "Let us go to the house of the Lord"? And if that was the case, and if Jesus was "eaten up" by his zeal for God's house, why wasn't I and most people whom I knew? Why did I often have such ambivalent feelings about worship, why did I so often go out of a sense of duty instead of eager anticipation? Was there something about me, or about the services, that kept me from being glad when the opportunity for worship presented itself?

When I asked myself, What was it I should expect to happen in church, the text of "Now the silence" came to me, giving me at least a number of reasons, any one of which should have made me glad to go to the house of the Lord. Used as an Entrance hymn, "Now the silence" could make the worshiper aware of what was going on in that "rare and royal meeting." When the hymn was accepted into a number of hymnals, I knew that others were engaged in the same struggle, and that hymnody could help to focus the attention of the worshiper on the purpose and meaning of worship.

Why then do I write hymns? To stir up my own awareness of God's will and mercy, to express my own need for him and to begin to render some genuine appreciation for his love, to review my place in his plan for me and for humanity, to refresh myself with his love so as to be able to feed others with it, to experience his forgiveness so that I can forgive others, to taste his peace so that I can be its instrument to others still at war with him, with themselves and one another, and to look forward to God's ultimate goal for me, for which I have been redeemed at so great a cost. And I have discovered that when a hymn succeeds in doing any of these things, it refreshes the spirit, redirects vision, soothes the soul, challenges to greater service, and offers genuine thanksgiving. Worship then is authentic and, I believe, pleasing and acceptable to God.

Ash Wednesday, 1987   J.J.V.

ORIGINAL HYMNS, CAROLS, AND SONGS

1   A COMET BLAZED ACROSS THE SKIES

A comet blazed across the skies
     above a sleeping, dying sphere,
just as a lost and hopeless race
saw its last lamplights disappear.

"Repent!" the angel-star proclaimed,
"Cling to the Savior God has sent;
this is the one true light of grace,
believe this Gospel and repent!"

Before that cry the idols crashed,
old chains were shattered, darkness cleft,
faith kindled, hope revived, and Christ
alone upon his throne was left.

For that bold angel we give thanks,
and for the Gospel he confessed,
his burning faith and legacy,
and for the freedom long suppressed.

In these last days of sore distress,
give us Your Star to see and heed,
that like the Magi we may find
the Savior we most crave and need.

LM (8.8.8.8.)

A mid the world's bleak wilderness
    A vineyard grows with promise green,
The planting of the Lord himself.

His love selected this terrain,
His vine with love he planted here
To bear the choicest fruit for him.

We are his branches, chosen, dear,
And though we feel the dresser's knife,
We are the objects of his care.

From him we draw the juice of life,
For him supply his winery
With fruit from which true joys derive.

Vine, keep what I was meant to be:
Your branch with your rich life in me.

Irregular

Before the marvel of this night,
 Adoring, fold your wings and bow,
Then tear the sky apart with light,
And with your news the world endow.
Proclaim the birth of Christ and peace,
That fear and death and sorrow cease:
Sing peace, sing peace, sing Gift of Peace,
 Sing peace, sing Gift of Peace!

Awake the sleeping world with song,
This is the day the Lord has made.
Assemble here, celestial throng,
In royal splendor come arrayed.
Give earth a glimpse of heavenly bliss,
A teasing taste of what they miss.
Sing bliss, sing bliss, sing endless bliss,
 Sing bliss, sing endless bliss!

The love that we have always known,
Our constant joy and endless light,
Now to the loveless world be shown,
Now break upon its deathly night.
Into one song compress the love
That rules our universe above:
Sing love, sing love, sing God is love,
 Sing love, sing God is love!

8.8.8.8.8.8.8.6.

B efore your awesome majesty,
    We humbly bow, we bend the knee
As to no merely earthly king,
Creator, Lord of everything.

Almighty, holy, unborn One,
Whose glory far outshines the sun:
Who can approach you and yet live,
Who dares to sin, and you forgive?

The oceans roar at your command,
You tame them when you raise your hand;
Into that sea you cast our sins,
With water our new life begins.

No God is there besides you, Lord,
No life is there without your Word;
Yet neither might nor glory move
Us to adore you as your love.

Beginning and the End are you,
To you all praise and thanks are due;
What stars and saints and angels see,
Grant us to share eternally.

LM (8.8.8.8.)

5 BEGIN THE SONG OF GLORY NOW

Begin the song of glory now:
  the Son has risen from his grave!
The night of mourning long is past;
life has a purpose, after all.
Our Samson smashed the gates of hell,
and we are free at last, at last!
Begin the song of glory now:
the Son has risen from our grave!

Prepare the song of glory now:
the Son has risen from his grave!
Composers, players, find new sounds
for every instrument and voice:
a note, a chord, an aria,
a Kyrie, a Gloria.
Prepare the song of glory now:
the Son has risen from our grave!

Repeat the song of glory now:
the Son has risen from his grave!
Complete the Easter overture,
and join the Alleluia choir.
"In Jesus' name" the song begin,
and end: "All praise to God alone!"
Repeat the song of glory now:
the Son has risen from our grave!

LMD (8.8.8.8.D)

6 CATCH THE VISION! SHARE THE GLORY!

Blessed children, saints, elect of God,
   Globe-encircling cloud of witnesses:
We have heard the Christmas angels,
We have seen the Easter sunrise,
Cried with joy when Christ began his reign.
   Catch the vision! Share the glory!
   Show the captives, tell them: Christ is here!

Universal Body of the Lord,
Chosen, called, made just, and glorified:
Ours the faith, and ours the triumph,
Ours the peace the world is seeking;
Who on earth as privileged as we?
   Catch the vision! Share the glory!
   Show the captives, tell them: Christ is here!

Heirs together of the grace of life,
All baptized into the death of Christ:
Born again, in love maturing,
From the altar free and cheerful,
Caring, winsome family of God.
   Catch the vision! Share the glory!
   Show the captives, tell them: Christ is here!

For this time and place have we been born,
Gifted by the Spirit, trained, and sent:
With the eyes of Jesus seeing,
With the hands of Jesus helping,
With the words of Jesus bringing life.
   Catch the vision! Share the glory!
   Show the captives, tell them: Christ is here!

9.9.8.8.9.8.9.

7 CHRIST GOES BEFORE

C hrist goes before, and we are called to follow,
    and all who follow find the Way, the Truth, the Life.

Where is that Way we near despaired of finding:
the way that comes from God and leads to God,
the realm where God is love and love is King,
a whole new order for a world astray?
Who wants to live where there's no love like this?
Is this the Kingdom we are ready for
    and desperate to find?

Christ goes before, and we are called to follow,
and all who follow find the Way, the Truth, the Life.

Where is that Truth we near despaired of knowing:
the truth that comes from God and leads to God,
the power to set us free, the power to change,
that faces Pilate and the cross and wins?
Who wants to live where there's no peace like this?
Is this the Power we are ready for
    and desperate to know?

Christ goes before, and we are called to follow,
and all who follow know the Way, the Truth, the Life.

Where is that Life we near despaired of having:
the life that comes from God and leads to God,
the hope of glory only Christ can give,
that shatters death and grief with Easter joy?
Who wants to live where there's no joy like this?
Is this the Glory we are ready for
    and desperate to have?

Christ goes before, and we are called to follow,
and all who follow have the Way, the Truth, the Life.

Irregular

8 COME, LORD JESUS, TO THIS PLACE

Come, Lord Jesus, to this place,
    Cheer it, fill it, with your grace;
Guest and friend, none more desired,
Bless the vows by you inspired.

Witness of this moment rare,
Free from sorrow, free from care;
For the years that lie ahead:
Promised joy and promised bread.

Seal the love that makes them one,
Love, their never-setting sun,
Love enough to face all fears,
Love enough to dry all tears.

As you love the Church, your Bride,
In such love may they abide;
As your Bride is bound to you,
Keep them faithful, Lord, and true.

7.7.7.7.

9 COUNT YOUR BLESSINGS, O MY SOUL

C ount your blessings, O my soul,
    For each one God's name extol,
See them all with Adam's eyes,
Every one a fresh surprise;
Splendors, glories everywhere,
Majesty beyond compare,
One and all his might declare.

Praise him, sky and sea and land,
Creatures exquisite and grand,
Who but God has power to spare,
Power to feed and love to care?
Everything he makes he keeps,
What he sows, he duly reaps,
What he watches, safely sleeps.

Time-bound creatures, praise the One
From whose hand the sun was spun;
Marvel that the Lord of earth
Chose to have a human birth,
In our time to live and die,
Thus our time to glorify,
Timeless now enthroned on high.

Wait no longer, heart and tongue,
Let the grateful song be sung;
Break into spontaneous praise
With the glee of holidays;
Start with nature's overture,
Add a chorus mightier,
Let the cosmic anthem soar!

7.7.7.7.7.7.7.

10   CREATOR, KEEPER, CARING LORD

C reator, Keeper, caring Lord
         Of all you deign to make,
Direct us toward your goal for us
With every breath we take:
In you we live, in you we move —
The ones you chose to love.

To faith and hope and love, dear God,
Add one more gift of grace:
Sound health of body, soul, and mind —
Your Spirit's dwelling place;
And should you let the body fail,
Keep mind and spirit well.

In wisdom let us guard the gift
Of wholeness you supply.
In mercy turn our ears and hands,
Like you, toward all who cry.
We know who heals our hurts and ills,
We know your gracious will.

Though far from perfect, we revere
Your earthly masterpiece:
The body Jesus shared and gave
To banish all disease,
That all who rise with him from death
May know the bliss of health.

8.6.8.6.8.6.

F ar from the time when we were few
   And left our homes abroad,
We stand today in blessing new
And rich before our God.

The seas were crossed, a home was found
Beside bright freedom's streams;
Your Word was planted, blessed, and crowned
Beyond our fathers' dreams.

Great miracles of service fill
Our memory so brief:
The wondrous working of a will
That conquers disbelief.

We stand before the world a proof
Of what God's grace can do
With children selfish and aloof
On whom the Spirit blew.

How much of this have we deserved?
How did we grasp the Truth?
How is the Good News still preserved
For us and for our youth?

New songs be made and work be done
In penitence and praise
For our amazing God, whose Son
Keeps smiling on our days.

CM (8.6.8.6.)

12   GATHER YOUR CHILDREN, DEAR SAVIOR, IN PEACE

Gather your children, dear Savior, in peace.
And draw us to you with your passionate pleas;
Still seek us and call us to come and be blessed,
To find in your arms, Lord, safety, comfort, and rest.

Knowing you, loving you, naming you Lord,
We cluster around you and grow by your Word,
One day to remember these moments so rare,
Of caring and closeness, just because you are there.

Love be our banner, forgiveness our theme,
Compassion our nature, your vision our dream;
Who knows what the Spirit of God yet can do,
What joy may be tasted, or what promise come true?

Host at our table in our house and yours,
Here bind us together with love that endures;
Like parents, like children, let this be our fame:
That, blessed, we bless many, to the praise of your name.

10.11.11.12.

13 GIVE GLORY, ALL CREATION

G ive glory, all creation,
　　Great seas and stars and blazing sun,
All join in adoration
Before the only holy One!
The God eternal name him,
The One who rules alone;
The King of kings acclaim him
Upon a heavenly throne!
No light exists without him,
No life but by his Word,
So gather, all, about him,
And own him our God, our Lord!
And own him our God, our Lord!

No realm is there so spacious,
No rule demanding greater might;
No one is there so gracious,
Yet just and holy, good and right;
Beyond all comprehension,
Beyond the last surprise,
Comes Love's divine invention:
This God for creatures dies!
No wonder angels praise him
And live in constant awe,
Should not all creatures raise him
An endless Alleluia!
An endless Alleluia!

7.8.7.8.7.6.7.6.7.6.7.7.7.

14   GO, MY CHILDREN, WITH MY BLESSING

G o, my children, with my blessing, never alone;
    Waking, sleeping, I am with you, you are my own;
In my love's baptismal river
I have made you mine forever,
Go, my children, with my blessing, you are my own.

Go, my children, sins forgiven, at peace and pure,
Here you learned how much I love you, what I can cure;
Here you heard my dear Son's story,
Here you touched him, saw his glory,
Go, my children, sins forgiven, at peace and pure.

Go, my children, fed and nourished, closer to me;
Grow in love and love by serving, joyful and free.
Here my Spirit's power filled you,
Here his tender comfort stilled you;
Go, my children, fed and nourished, joyful and free.

I the Lord will bless and keep you, and give you peace,
I the Lord will smile upon you, and give you peace;
I the Lord will be your Father,
Savior, Comforter, and Brother:
Go, my children, I will keep you, and give you peace.

8.4.8.4.8.8.8.4.

15 GOD OF THE SPARROW

G of the sparrow
   God of the whale
God of the swirling stars
    How does the creature say Awe
    How does the creature say Praise

God of the earthquake
God of the storm
God of the trumpet blast
    How does the creature cry Woe
    How does the creature cry Save

God of the rainbow
God of the cross
God of the empty grave
    How does the creature say Grace
    How does the creature say Thanks

God of the hungry
God of the sick
God of the prodigal (wayward child)
    How does the creature say Care
    How does the creature say Life

God of the neighbor
God of the foe
God of the pruning hook (olive branch)
    How does the creature say Love
    How does the creature say Peace

God of the ages
God near at hand
God of the loving heart
    How do your children say Joy
    How do your children say Home

5.4.6.7.7.

16 GOD, WHO BUILT THIS WONDROUS PLANET

God, who built this wondrous planet
   And all worlds beyond these bounds,
Crown your work and ours with blessing,
Meet us here on hallowed ground.
With your glory fill this temple,
Here be sought and here be found.

Christ, you build a holy structure
That, like you, outlasts the earth;
Chosen, like yourself, you make us
Living stones of priceless worth;
Home, where prodigals returning,
Celebrate with holy mirth.

Spirit, make your church a beacon
Beaming hope where hoping wanes,
Daily in these stones creating
Life where death no longer reigns,
And in grateful hearts forgiven
Spark the love the world but feigns.

Living Father, living children,
Living servants, living Lord;
Living Savior, living Body,
Living members, living Word;
Living Spirit, living temple:
We adoring, you adored!

8.7.8.7.8.7.

17 HERE IS THE LIVING PROOF, GOOD LORD

Here is the living proof, good Lord,
of what our faith can do;
see what our efforts can achieve
when they are blessed by You.

This house we hallowed to Your name,
where swallows make their home,
where those are blessed who meet You here
and pray, "Your kingdom come!"

You, Jesus, are the living proof
that all our debts are paid,
that all we owed and could not pay
on You, God's Lamb, were laid.

You carried every debt we owed
to cross and death and grave,
and so what we could never pay
You graciously forgave.

Make us the living proof, good Lord,
of what Your Word can do,
to show the world the Way, the Truth,
and Life that come from You.

To all whose debts to You are paid
You set forth one more goal:
"Owe no one anything but love"
till all the world is whole.

Great triune God, inhabit us
and fill us with Your grace,
that we who meet You in this house
may one day see Your face!

CM

18 HOW COULD I HURT YOU SO

How could I hurt you so,
 whom once I called my friend,
forgetful of my pledge to you,
your gifts misspent!
For you I thirst,
my bones are dry,
and I am as you found me first.

How could you love me so,
whom once you called your friend,
forgetful of my faithlessness
for years on end?
I claim no grace,
but for your cross
restore my joy in your embrace.

6.6.8.4.4.4.8.

19 HOW MEAGER AND MUNDANE

How meager and mundane
    our view of heaven is
before we see God's majesty
or we are his;
So lift your eyes,
my soul, and see
the sapphire throne and realms of bliss!

How futile and morose
our daily life must grow
when all we have is what we grasp
down here below;
so set your heart,
my soul, on things
above where lasting treasures glow!

How aimless and ingrown
our pilgrimage becomes
when in this passing place we build
our lasting homes;
so set your feet,
my soul, upon
the road to yon palatial domes!

6.6.8.4.4.4.8.

How pleasant, Lord, when brothers live
   in peace and unity,
when in your children your own love
the world can feel and see.

But we confess our wanton ways,
no one is innocent;
who has not sinned, has not forgiven?
Our fellowship is rent.

In shame and near despair we cry,
have mercy, Lord, forgive!
Unworthy all, we claim your grace,
then judge if we should live.

Repair the fabric of your church
which we have torn apart,
the garment of your peace and love,
as living as your heart.

Accusing falsely, wrongly hurt,
we sulk the years away,
suspicious of each other's aims,
we cannot even pray.

The whitening harvest waits and rots,
the sheaves we bring are small;
your judgment clock moves fast to strike,
we slumber through your call.

Bind up the fractures, heal the wounds
that break your heart and ours;
speak your strong reconciling word,
restore our waning powers.

Upon your dear afflicted Bride
come place your healing hand;
renew the love we once avowed
and make us one again.

CM (8.6.8.6.)

21   I PRAISE YOU, LORD, IN EVERY HOUR

I praise you, Lord, in every hour
　With all my power,
Since you have heard my crying;
Your arm has vanquished all my foes
With all their woes,
Their victory denying.
Dear God, I plead
From my deep need,
And to my cries
Your mercy flies;
Your grace relieves my sighing.

Praise God, all you who call him Lord,
He keeps his word:
Remember how he saved you.
His anger lasts a moment brief,
Soon comes relief;
You know that he forgave you.
Your holy god
Withdraws his rod;
You go to bed,
Your eyes still red,
But waken free and joyful.

Lord, you are patient, I am weak,
Until I seek,
And then I find you waiting;
You build my confidence and strength,
And I, at length,
See all my fears abating.
How should I not
Praise you, my God?
Your life I see
Begun in me,
New joy and hope creating.

8.4.7.8.4.7.4.4.4.4.7.

22 IN HOPELESSNESS AND NEAR DESPAIR

In hopelessness and near despair,
I cry to you, my Savior!
My guilt is more than I can bear,
I have not earned your favor.
You know me as I really am:
How much is truth, how much is sham;
Why should you heed my pleading?

I see my heart's condition now,
My heart's diverse affections.
Why do I love the things you loathe;
I'm torn in two directions:
Now prodigal, now pharisee,
O God, be merciful to me;
Who else but you can help me?

I tremble as I feel your hand,
Expecting retribution,
Yet hear no curse or reprimand,
But grace and absolution:
With you there is forgiveness, Lord,
You speak the sweet, consoling word,
And I am sure you love me!

Forgiven, free of guilt and shame,
Grant me some time to render
A gift to glorify your name,
Love to reflect your splendor:
This world must know what I have learned,
That you bestow what none has earned:
The joy of full forgiveness!

8.7.8.7.8.8.7.

L et us praise our gracious God,
    Children of an alien sod:
He has made this dwelling place
Haven for a scattered race:
Alleluia.

Sons and daughters, greatly blessed,
Of a nation much oppressed,
Like our fathers, so may we
Seize the Gospel hungrily:
Alleluia.

Precious altar, precious font,
Food and life for every want:
Here our parents, here may we
Hear the truth that makes us free:
Alleluia.

Here a hundred years have passed,
And His promises still last;
For a thousand more we pray,
And new mercies every day:
Alleluia.

God outreaching, God enfleshed,
God of life, in life enmeshed,
Fatherly, delightfully
Gracious Holy Trinity!
Alleluia.

7.7.7.7. and Alleluia

24   LORD, AS YOU TAUGHT US ONCE TO PRAY

L ord, as you taught us once to pray
    So teach us now in love to live.
From heaven you brought the better way,
You sought us lost and fugitive.
You changed our wills from "must" to "may,"
You calm us with your "I forgive,"
And all our fears are soothed away.
It is by love that we survive.
Lord, as you taught us once to pray,
So teach us now in love to live.

As you for love were crucified,
So teach us, Lord, that way to peace.
You healed the hurts of those who cried,
You made the griefs of mourners cease,
Gave Satan's prey a place to hide.
Who sees you on your cross-bound knees,
Sees love that cannot be denied.
This kind of love in us increase.
As you for love were crucified,
So teach us, Lord, that way to peace.

As you were moved by love toward man,
Make us such vessels of your grace.
We need no other reason than
That we reflect our Father's face.
Show us the depth and height and span
Of love that spares no sacrifice,
And we shall do what you began:
Reach to the world with your embrace.
As you were moved by love toward man,
Make us such vessels of your grace.

Lord, as in love you saw God's will,
So make that love, that will, ours too.
This world in endless dryness still
Will die and dies without your dew.
Since God is love, and angels thrill
To find this wonder ever new,
His gracious will help us fulfill
And join his joyful retinue.
Lord, as in love you saw God's will,
So make that love, that will, ours too.

10 lines of 8'

25   LORD, I MUST PRAISE YOU

L ord, I must praise you when I stand in wonder
    At your mighty works and splendor.
There is no other God, no one above you,
Yet so close to those who love you.
O Lord, have mercy!
All your works declare your majesty
In an endless grand doxology;
Even more would I praise
Your compassion, love, and grace.
O Lord, have mercy!

Nothing but good you give to those who fear you,
Ever near those who revere you.
To you the hungry come for daily feeding,
And the poor for justice pleading.
O Lord, have mercy!
All your deeds are honest and sincere,
All your vows as true as they appear;
Perfect love, rarest kind,
All I need in you I find.
Lord, have mercy!

You sent your people long-desired salvation,
Making us a blessed nation.
You are the Rock: on you our hopes are founded,
Safe we dwell, by love surrounded.
O Lord, have mercy!
Make us wise to follow in your ways,
And receive our sacrifice of praise.
We are yours, yours to use
For your dream as you may choose.
O Lord, have mercy!

Irregular

26 NOW, AT THE PEAK OF WONDER

Now, at the peak of wonder,
  Sing your new song of praise,
Tell all the world He loves you,
Lord of your years and days.
Caught by His glory, shine with its splendor,
Now, while your heart's ablaze.

For the sad world around you,
Helpless and terrified,
Dying for want of rescue,
Watching you from outside:
Here is the water, here is the banquet,
Here is the Lamb that died.

Garden of children growing,
Help those who crawl to walk,
Feed them the Bread from heaven,
Teach those who lisp to talk:
Tell them the story, show them the glory,
Sheep of the Shepherd's flock.

Make this a place so winsome
Jesus is almost seen,
Sinners and angels searching,
Find here a joy serene:
Filled with the Spirit, glow with the glory,
Glory of pastures green.

Now at the Savior's impulse
Touch with His healing hand
All those who suffer, hunger,
Mourn, or wear Satan's brand.
Friend to the lonely, God's earthly angels,
Strong with the wronged to stand.

Now to the caring Father,
Now to the risen Son,
Now to the cheering Spirit,
Now to the Holy One:
Sing alleluias, live alleluias,
Never the song be done!

7.7.7.7.5.5.6

27 NOW THE SILENCE

N ow the silence
   Now the peace
Now the empty hands uplifted

Now the kneeling
Now the plea
Now the Father's arms in welcome

Now the hearing
Now the power
Now the vessel brimmed for pouring

Now the Body
Now the Blood
Now the joyful celebration

Now the wedding
Now the songs
Now the heart forgiven leaping

Now the Spirit's visitation
Now the Son's epiphany
Now the Father's blessing

Now   Now   Now

Irregular

O day of days, the day I found
   The love that had been seeking me;
More than a word, more than a sound,
That Word was God and set me free.

O day of days, the day I found
That Word a body on a cross;
No sacrifice of friend has bound
Me to him by so great a loss.

O day of days, the day I found
A life to live that's more than me,
A blessing for the world around,
A cause to serve, a way to be.

O day of days, the day I found
Your people raised like me to sing;
Now one with them and those beyond
I look for ways to thank our King.

Stand by me, Father, Flesh, and Flame:
Embrace, embolden and increase
Your child reborn to bear Your name,
Another messenger of peace.

LM (8.8.8.8.)

29   O GOD, ETERNAL FATHER, LORD

O God, eternal Father, Lord,
    Creator by your mighty Word,
Be now by us and all adored. Alleluia.

O Son, still God today as then,
In flesh like ours you dwelled with men,
Here served and died and rose again. Alleluia.

O Spirit, God, Iconoclast,
By Blood and Water cleanse our past,
The life you seed, make grow and last. Alleluia.

8.8.8. and Alleluia

30 PASS IN REVIEW

Pass in review, ambassador of Christ:
    Pass in review, each sacrifice and prize,
Pass in review, the sowings of the Word,
Pass in review, the harvest gleaned and stored.

Vessel of clay for mysteries divine,
Chosen to join the apostolic line,
Given your heritage, your gifts, your call,
Your place as sentinel on Zion's wall.

Servant of sinners, though yourself the same,
Partner in sorrow, yet with hope aflame,
Cheering the lonely, Gospeling the poor,
Leading your precious flock through Christ the Door.

Pass in review, slaves ransomed and set free,
Pass in review, one noble company,
Pass in review, your victor's banner raise,
Pass in review, your life a song of praise.

10.10.10.10.

31   PEACE CAME TO EARTH

P eace came to earth at last that chosen night
     When angels clove the sky with song and light
And God embodied love and sheathed his might —
    Who could but gasp: Immanuel!
    Who could but sing: Immanuel!

And who could be the same for having held
The infant in their arms, and later felt
The wounded hands and side, all doubts dispelled —
    Who could but sigh: Immanuel!
    Who could but shout: Immanuel!

You show the Father none has ever seen,
In flesh and blood you bore our griefs and pain,
In bread and wine you visit us again —
    Who could but see Immanuel!
    Who could but thrill: Immanuel!

How else could I have known you, O my God!
How else could I have loved you, O my God!
How else could I embrace you, O my God!
    Who could but pray: Immanuel!
    Who could but praise Immanuel!

10.10.10.8.8.

S ee this wonder in the making:
   God himself this child is taking
As a lamb safe in his keeping,
His to be, awake or sleeping.

Miracle each time it happens,
As the door to heaven opens
And the Father beams: "Beloved,
Heir of gifts a king would covet!"

Far more tender than a mother,
Far more caring than a father,
God, into your arms we place him,
With your love and peace embrace him.

Here we bring a child of nature,
Home we take a newborn creature,
Now God's precious son or daughter,
Born again by Word and Water.

NOTE: For female infants, substitute *her* for *him* in stanza 3; for multiple baptisms, substitute *each* for *this* in stanza 1, and *them* for *him* in stanza 3.

LM (8.8.8.8.) Trochaic

33 THEN THE GLORY

Then the glory
  Then the rest
Then the sabbath peace unbroken

Then the garden
Then the throne
Then the crystal river flowing

Then the splendor
Then the life
Then the new creation singing

Then the marriage
Then the love
Then the feast of joy unending

Then the knowing
Then the light
Then the ultimate adventure

Then the Spirit's harvest gathered
Then the Lamb in majesty
Then the Father's Amen

Then   Then   Then

Irregular

T his child of ours
   —This miracle —
God has a dream and plan for it:
He washes it,
He cradles it,
He blesses it and calls it His:
　　This child of ours,
　　This child of God.

This child of God
—This miracle —
Reborn of water and the Word:
The Book of Life
Records its name,
God smiles and angels celebrate:
　　This child of ours,
　　This child of God.

This child of ours
—This miracle —
Whom Christ would die for, we may love,
And train and raise,
And teach and praise,
And watch the Spirit mold a life:
　　This child of ours,
　　This child of God.

8.8.8.8. Refrain

35 THIS IS A TIME FOR BANNERS AND BELLS

This is a time for banners and bells,
    For trumpets and festive throngs;
This is a time for holiday frills,
For worship and marching songs:
        Come, sing to the Lord,
        Give thanks to the Lord,
        For he makes all things new,
        For he makes all things new.

Think of the time when we were alone,
A nobody, weak and small,
Christ sought us out and made us his own,
The Bride of the Lord of all:
        Come, sing to the Lord . . .

Cherish the time we spent in his grace,
The ones with the dream and we,
Sheltered and fed and loved in this place
By him who has made us free:
        Come, sing to the Lord . . .

Live for the time of glory to come,
His pennant of love unfurled,
Cross-bearing pilgrims, heading for home,
Whose faith overcomes the world:
        Come, sing to the Lord . . .

+ Gloria Dei, Christ is alive,
    And we, his beloved Bride,
    Creature so rare, now seventy-five,
    A diamond he wears with pride:
        Come, sing to the Lord . . .

+ (stanza optional)

9.7.9.7. Refrain

36 THIS LOVE, O CHRIST

This love, O Christ, is so much like your own,
This love of husband for his wife:
A new creation molded into one,
Self-giving, sharing bread and breath,
No sacrifice too great, not even death,
One love, one promise, one for all of life.

This love, O Church, is so much like your own,
This love of bride for her dear groom:
A new creation molded into one,
Devoted, faithful unto death,
Entwined together like a living wreath,
To scent this life with love's divine perfume.

10.8.10.8.10.10.

37 THIS TOUCH OF LOVE

This touch of love,
     this taste of peace,
how can it last and still increase?
I cannot bear
to have this air
of wonder cease.

This happy feast,
this friendly bond,
how can I keep it long beyond
this fleeting hour,
this surge of power,
this treasure found?

This glow of joy,
this glimpse of light,
this momentary pure delight,
I dread to leave
to fret and grieve
and die in night.

This freshly washed,
this feeling free,
I need to know that this can be;
make me believe
what I receive
is meant for me.

Christ Jesus, you
are what I need,
the Bread and Wine on which I feed,
no friend so true,
no life so new —
I'm rich indeed.

O Savior, now
my spirit raise,
give new direction to my ways,
in all I view,
in all I do,
to give you praise.

4.4.8.4.4.4.

Though mountains quake and oceans roar
And lightning cracks the heavens,
Though nations rage in ruthless war,
We still have one last haven:
Our God still is God;
High above the flood,
This God's in control
From pole to trembling pole:
The Lord of hosts is with us.

There is a city where God dwells,
Where peace flows like a river;
Beyond the reach of death and hell,
It stands secure forever.
There, held in his arm,
Like sheep safe from harm,
All promises kept,
Yes, even while we slept:
So great a Savior loved us!

Attention, nations, friend and foe:
Hear God himself appealing:
All who are tired of hate and woe,
Come to his Son for healing!
What we could not do,
Live and hope anew,
The Devil's head crushed,
Our every terror hushed,
God does, and he is with us!

8.7.8.7.6.6.6.6.7.

Up through endless ranks of angels,
  Cries of triumph in his ears,
To his heavenly throne ascending,
Having vanquished all their fears,
Christ looks down upon his faithful,
Leaving them in happy tears.

Death-destroying, life-restoring,
Proven Equal to our need,
Now for us before the Father
As our brother intercede:
Flesh that for our world was wounded,
Living, for the wounded plead.

To our lives of wanton wandering
Send your promised Spirit-Guide,
Through our lives of fear and failure
With your power and love abide:
Welcome us, as you were welcomed,
To an endless Eastertide.

Alleluia, alleluia,
Oh, to breathe the Spirit's grace!
Alleluia, alleluia,
Oh, to see the Father's face!
Alleluia, alleluia,
Oh, to feel the Son's embrace!

8.7.8.7.8.7.

Where shepherds lately knelt,
    and kept the angel's word,
I come in half-belief,
a pilgrim strangely stirred;
but there is room
and welcome there
for me.

In that unlikely place
I find him as they said:
sweet newborn Babe, how frail!
and in a manger bed:
a still small Voice
to cry one day
for me.

How should I not have known
Isaiah would be there,
his prophecies fulfilled?
With pounding heart, I stare:
a Child, a Son,
the Prince of Peace —
for me.

Can I, will I forget
how Love was born and burned
its way into my heart —
unasked, unforced, unearned,
to die, to live,
and not alone
for me?

12.12.10.10.

41 WHERE YOU ARE, THERE IS LIFE

Where you are, there is life:
    the cosmic "Let there be!"
the "Lazarus, come forth!"
Without you nothing is or grows,
your Word umbilical to all.
Where you are, there is life —
    and you are here!

Where you are, there is love:
a promise made and kept,
one Son who dies for all,
a love that banishes all fear,
that, like its Father, never ends.
Where you are, there is love —
    and you are here!

Where you are, there is peace:
a resting place at last,
no running anymore;
forgiven and forgiving friends,
the quest of all who share your plan.
Where you are, there is peace —
    and you are here!

True life and love and peace
you are, and we are yours,
Creator, Lamb, and Dove.
Make us partakers of your dream,
see what your heart and hands have done,
and smile and say again:
    how good, how good!

6.6.6.8.8.6.4.

42 WHO COULD HAVE DREAMT A LAND LIKE THIS?

Who could have dreamt a land like this,
    The answer to an exile's prayer,
An Eden in the making?
The thankful find a rare surprise,
Bright bursts of blessing everywhere,
At every new dawn's breaking.
Ring out, sing out,
Hills replying, banners flying,
Bells a-ringing,
Flood our Father's throne with singing.

In deep and honest grief lament
Your glory marred by greed and pride,
The blood for vengeance crying.
Before the Crucified repent
The wasted land, the fratricide,
Your ruthless, selfish vying.
Toll then, toll ten
Bells of mourning, wrath and warning,
Tearful token,
Once for each commandment broken.

God's grace and power remain the same
As when our fathers found this shore,
His Spirit for the asking.
America, invoke that Name,
So shall we all, spared want and war,
In fruitful peace be basking.
Sing out, ring out,
Live in thrilling, dream-fulfilling
Expectation.
Crack new bells in jubilation!

Irregular

43   WHO IS THIS WHO COMES FROM NOWHERE?

Who is this who comes from nowhere,
    claims to be the Son of God,
says: "I am the true Messiah,
you can end your waiting now.
Is it love you want — I show it,
is it peace you need — I give it,
is it joy you crave — I vow it,
you can end your seeking now.

"Search instead the sacred Record,
trace my life from crib to cross,
hear me preaching love and freedom,
calling all to God's own cause.
See me give my life for sinners,
see me rise again triumphant,
see me prove God's lovingkindness:
what more can the Savior do?"

See the cosmic plan unfolding,
meant for all to have a part;
someone must believe and play it,
if God's will is to be done.
Someone must continue teaching,
someone must continue serving,
someone must be bold and faithful,
if the kingdom is to come.

Blessed then the poor in spirit,
blest the mournful and the meek,
blest the merciful and righteous,
blest the pure who work for peace.
Patience! we shall stand in glory
thrilled to hear our throned Messiah:
"Welcome, blessed of my Father,
now the joy-full life begins!"

8.7.8.7.8.8.8.7.   Copyright © 1987 by Jaroslav J. Vajda

44   YOU ARE THE KING

Y ou are the King Isaiah saw adored
      By flaming angels 'round Your lofty throne;
In reverent awe they chorus to their Lord
An endless "Holy, holy, holy One!"

But woe to me! I cannot join that choir;
No sinner can behold that sight and live.
Unclean before that all-consuming Fire,
I cannot be forgiven or forgive.

To my surprise, You stretch Your loving hand
To cleanse my heart, my lips, my eyes, my ears;
You touch me, me! and I see how You spanned
And crossed the gaping gulf to make me Yours.

You call me, Holy Trinity, to be
Your earthly angel? Here am I, send me!

14 lines of 10′

45   YOU ARE THE ROCK

You are the Rock, and we were hewn
    From You, eternal and triune.
To build Your holy Temple here
You chose the tenting pioneer,
Your Spirit setting one by one
As living stone on living stone,
And so this House was raised by You.

Begotten by Your word of grace,
Behold Your family and race:
Its members each a wondrous birth,
Your love embodied here on earth,
One holy, growing miracle.
Add living cell to living cell
Until Your Body fills the world.

As You have blessed us all these years,
Forgiving sins, removing fears,
So may we live as grateful heirs,
Invest the faith that once was theirs,
Your living Word our food and drink.
Add living link to living link
Until the chain of love is forged.

Elect of God, whom God so loved,
Remember how that love was proved;
Elect of God, redeemed by Christ,
Rejoice to be so highly prized;
Elect of God, the Spirit's pride,
Reach out to all who stand outside,
And crown the work so well begun.

8.7.8.7.8.8.7.

46 YOU ARE THE SHEPHERD

You are the Shepherd, we your sheep
   By Water and the Word;
The promises you make you keep,
And all our cries are heard.

The fearful, helpless, old, and tired
Are cast upon your care
And on the ones whom you inspired
Your love and cheer to share.

What honor and what joy to be
Your hands, your feet, your mind,
To know what makes your children free,
The peace they seek to find.

Bless what we are and what we do,
Good Shepherd, best of friends,
That all your sheep may share with you
The life that never ends.

CM (8.6.8.6.)

47 YOU, JESUS, ARE MY SHEPHERD TRUE

Y ou, Jesus, are my Shepherd true,
    And I your sheep quite helpless;
My ever-loving Guide are you,
Your every thought is selfless;
You feed me, guard me, lead the way
To peace at night and joy by day:
I frolic in your favor.

I follow you. The path you choose,
It is the best way for me;
The lamb you love you will not lose,
You walk the way before me;
And though I pass through death's dark vale,
It is my Lord's familiar trail:
I know its glorious ending.

Surrounded when I am by foes
Who scorn me or ignore me,
In your strong arms I find repose;
You spread a feast before me!
You welcome me! I find a place
Of honor as your heir of grace,
At home with you forever.

8.7.8.7.8.8.7.

SERIES A

Second Sunday of Easter   *Acts 2:14a, 22-32*

The One who died by sinners' hands
On brutal Calvary
Was God's own Son, confirmed by death,
To set us sinners free.

So sure was David of his hope
That his great Son would rise,
He lived and died sure that he too
Would live in Paradise.

Doxology:
Now sing the mighty acts of God,
Now make his mercy known,
Now mark the triumph of his love,
Now gather round his throne.

The risen Christ, the ruling King,
The coming Judge and Lord,
Be welcomed, praised, obeyed, and served,
And evermore adored.

Third Sunday of Easter   *Acts 2:14a, 36-47*

The Man we crucified is made
By God the Lord of all;
He chose this way to justify
The victims of the Fall.

What shall we do to show our true
Repentance for this crime?
Be cleansed by him and tell his love
Until the end of time.

Doxology:

Fourth Sunday of Easter   *Acts 6:1-9; 7:2a, 51-60*

The kingdom, like a mustard seed,
Began with just a few,
But these, devoted to their Lord,
Miraculously grew.

And other seeds, like Stephen, fell
Into the ground to die,
But from them sprang a line of trees
Whose branches touch the sky.

Doxology:

Fifth Sunday of Easter   *Acts 17:1-15*

First to the Jews and then the Greeks
Christ's messengers proclaimed
The Risen Savior of the world,
By God himself acclaimed.

And some believed, and some did not,
And some just turned away,
But those who took the word to heart
Found their own Easter Day.

Doxology:

Sixth Sunday of Easter   *Acts 17:22-31*

All have a god whom they revere,
To whom they give their due,
But Christ has come to show the One
Whom we proclaim to you.

He is the Father of mankind
And of a Son divine,
Who, though a man, will judge all men,
Whom no grave can confine.

Doxology:

Seventh Sunday of Easter   *Acts 1:(1-7) 8-14*

This parting word the Savior spoke
To his assembled band:
"Go forth and make me followers
In this and every land.

"Baptize and teach what I have taught,
And I will be with you!"
With this he raised his hands and rose,
And disappeared from view.

Doxology:

Text reprinted by permission from Easter Motet Series A, copyright © 1986 Augsburg Publishing House.

SERIES B

Second Sunday of Easter   *Acts 3:13-15, 17-26*

God's power still indwelling him,
Bold Peter dares Christ's foes:
"How could you kill the Prince of Life,
Whom Abraham's God chose?

But God restored him back to life —
And you can still repent;
This time accept with grateful hearts
The Gift that God has sent."

Doxology:
O Spirit of the Risen Christ,
O Savior, Victor, Friend,
O smiling Father, ever our
Beginning and our End.

Combine our song of worship with
Your angel choirs, that when
We reach your presence we may join
Their glorious Amen!

Third Sunday of Easter   *Acts 4:8-12*

> The courts of evil still condemn
> The guiltless Son of Man;
> So will it be, so is it now,
> And was since time began.
>
> Before Christ's judges Peter stands
> For healing one born lame,
> Proclaiming that salvation comes
> By none but Jesus' name.
>
> *Doxology:*

Fourth Sunday of Easter   *Acts 4:23-33*

> As Christ, their Master, once condemned,
> Was by the grave released,
> So Peter, John, could not be held
> By prison or high priest.
>
> They had to tell what God had done
> And what he still can do,
> To make the Gospel known to all:
> That Word makes all things new.
>
> *Doxology:*

Fifth Sunday of Easter   *Acts 8:26-40*

> Not for Jerusalem and Jew
> Alone did Jesus die;
> Go, Philip, greet the African
> And give him God's reply.
>
> Isaiah pictures God's meek lamb
> For sinners sacrificed,
> And sinners recognizing him
> Would ask to be baptized.
>
> *Doxology:*

Sixth Sunday of Easter   *Acts 11:19-30*

> The blood of martyrs is not shed
> In vain, but sows the seeds
> Of valiant new disciples whom
> The world wants not but needs.
>
> Death turns to life, and scorn to praise,
> By God's strange alchemy;
> The Gospel fathers a new breed
> Of heavenly ancestry.

Doxology:

Seventh Sunday of Easter   *Acts 1:15-26*

> The chosen Twelve, now lacking one,
> Met to replace their loss;
> In prayer they sought the will of him
> Whose throne replaced the cross.
>
> To prove his care for every need,
> He made their number whole,
> So all who take each step with him
> Will reach their glorious goal.

Doxology:

Text reprinted by permission from Easter Motet Series B, copyright © 1984 Augsburg Publishing House.

SERIES C

Second Sunday of Easter   *Acts 5:12, 17-32*

> How futile of the grave to try
> To hold the rising Lord!
> How useless of his enemies
> To chain the living Word!
>
> Both tomb and prison must release
> That race divinely born;
> For those obeying God, not men,
> Each day's an Easter morn.

Doxology:
With pulsing, full, and bursting heart,
Repeat the Easter song,
The new life celebrate, the feast
Of victory prolong!

The Father of all life be praised,
The Son who vanquished death,
The Spirit, making all things new,
Adore with every breath!

Third Sunday of Easter   *Acts 9:1-20*

Saul heard the cry we all must hear
Before we come to faith:
"Why do you hound me, little one?
Why do you cause my death?"

But when we cry in turn, "O Lord,
What will you have me do?"
He comes in mercy, "Peace!" he says,
"I want to make you new."

Doxology:

Fourth Sunday of Easter   *Acts 13:15, 16a, 26-33*

God's promises have never failed,
The Word he speaks holds true,
And whether we believe or not,
God does what he must do.

The faithless Jews reject their Christ,
Fulfilling his true word,
While all believing Israel
Is proud to call him Lord.

Doxology:

Fifth Sunday of Easter   *Acts 13:44-52*

The Gospel, like a passing cloud,
Is meant to shower all,
Christ made his sacrifice for each
Lost victim of the Fall.

The Spirit lingers only where
His gift is well received,
Where, on the cross, despite the shame,
One's Savior is perceived.

Doxology:

Sixth Sunday of Easter   *Acts 14:8-18*

How like two gods th' apostles seem,
With healing powers endowed;
Yet knowing where they got the gift,
They glorify their God.

In flesh the Son of God appeared,
Here founded his domain;
He chooses vessels made of clay
To magnify his reign.

Doxology:

Seventh Sunday of Easter   *Acts 16:6-10*

A voice from Macedonia
Cries: "Come and help us, please!"
And lo, the praying man is heard
While still upon his knees.

No other plea so pleases God
As when his children cry;
Will he not answer them at once
And to their rescue fly?

Doxology:

49 GIFT OF JOY

Gift of Joy — for a people steeped in restless gloom,
   Gift of God — would it ever come?
Suddenly, in the night, bursting through the skies,
   See the promised Dawn arise!

Gift of Peace — for a people paralyzed with fear,
Gift of God — how would it appear?
Suddenly, in the night, bursting through the skies,
   See the promised Dawn arise!

Gift of Love, Gift of Grace, Gift of Hope and Life
For a people tired of strife.
Suddenly, in the night, bursting through the skies,
   See the promised Dawn arise!

Irregular

I have a Father you would like
  To be your Father, too.
There's no one like Him in the world
To do what He can do.

He understands me when I cry,
and when I'm all alone;
He lets me know He's there nearby
As well as on His throne.

My Father is a King, you see,
The greatest King of all,
And yet when His own Son was born,
He shared a cattle stall.

He came because He cares for me,
And so He loves you, too.
Do you know any other friend
Who'd live and die for you?

Now wouldn't you like to be God's child,
With Jesus as your Friend,
Someone who cares so much for you,
Whose love will never end?

CM (8.6.8.6.)

51   O DEAREST FRIEND

O dearest Friend, my nearest and most faithful Friend,
    Do not discard me though I grieve you much.
I look for you at every cliff-walled trail's end,
In crowds and lonely rooms, to feel your touch.
I mourn the vows of love I made but have not kept,
I call you from a heart you made your own.
Remember me as one who in the Garden slept
While you were on your way to earn my fadeless crown.

Create in me a heart as clean as newest born,
A heart, my God, that beats for you alone;
Make it a temple your free Spirit would adorn,
With living flesh replace my heart of stone.
Restore to me the joy of your salvation,
Recapture, oh, the thrill of our first love,
Securely hold me, mold me your creation,
Delight me yet again with such disarming love.

12.10.12.10.12.10.12.12.

52   ROCK-A-BYE, MY DEAR LITTLE BOY

Rock-a-bye, my dear little Boy, dear little Boy,
   Wonder of wonders, my blessing and joy:
Slumber as I gently hold you,
Let my tender love enfold you,
Gift of God to me and the world,
Here in my arms lies so peacefully curled.

Little Jesus, Infant divine, Infant divine,
One with the Father, yet born to be mine:
As I rock you calmly sleeping,
Angel guards their watch are keeping;
Precious Child, one day we shall see
What love has destined for you and for me.

12.10.8.8.8.10.

(New text for Czech carol "Hajej, nynjej," commonly known as *ROCKING*)

53 SOMEONE SPECIAL

S omeone Special, I know who:
    That Someone, my God, is You!
Who could make a world like this
And a heaven full of bliss;
Someone special I must be,
Since You made it all for me!

Someone Special, that You are,
To create the Christmas Star,
Heralding the Savior's birth,
Bringing peace and joy to earth.
Someone special I must be,
Since You made that Star for me!

Someone Special, who would give
His own Son that all might live,
And by Him would set us free
From all sin and misery.
Someone special I must be,
Since You gave Your Son for me!

Someone Special, who would send
His good Spirit for a Friend,
Faith Creator, Light and Guide,
Always standing at my side.
Someone special I must be,
Since You gave that Gift to me!

Someone Special — God and man,
You were there when I began,
You'll be there when I depart,
For You live within my heart.
Someone special — now I see,
That someone is really me.

7.7.7.7.7.7.

The friend I need
is the friend I have
when I have You for a friend;
who else would bleed
out of selfless love
and stay my friend to the end?

"I call you friends,"
says the Son of God,
"to tell you how much you are worth."
The Father sends
what no one else could:
his gift of peace to the earth.

I look at You
whom I call my friend,
to know what friendship should be;
now born anew
like the Child God sent,
I start to be what I see.

I look around
with my newborn eyes
and see so many alone.
The love I found
and the Lord I prize
can draw us all into one.

4.5.7.4.5.7.

TRANSLATIONS

Slovak Hymns

Slovak Carols and Songs

German Hymns

German Carols and Anthems

Hungarian Hymns

Slovak Hymns

55 ASCENDING, CHRIST RETURNS TO GOD

1. Ascending, Christ returns to God: Alleluia.
   That we may go the way he trod: Alleluia.

2. He wears the crown of victory: Alleluia.
   From doom and death he set us free: Alleluia.

3. At his most glorious festival: Alleluia.
   Sing, faithful Christians, one and all: Alleluia.

4. Remember how he told his own: Alleluia.
   I go to my dear Father's throne: Alleluia.

5. Do not depart Jerusalem: Alleluia.
   Until the promised Spirit come: Alleluia.

6. Until you learn all you must know: Alleluia.
   To teach the word and where to go: Alleluia.

7. Without his aid you cannot do: Alleluia.
   What I your Lord assign to you: Alleluia.

8. So kindle, Lord, the Spirit's flame: Alleluia.
   And thaw our lives to praise your name: Alleluia.

9. Until with you, when life is done: Alleluia.
   We share the glory you have won: Alleluia.

8.4.8.4.

56 CHRISTIANS, LET US REMEMBER

1. Christians, let us remember
   Our precious legacy,
   And see how we may honor
   Our debt most fittingly,
   Recalling those who cleansed us
   From pagan ways of death
   And brought us to the bosom
   Of our most holy faith.

2. For what should one most covet—
   Good fortune, fame, or this:
   To bear the name of Christian
   And claim a certain bliss;
   To know the saving Gospel
   That multiplies on earth
   Faith, hope, and love eternal:
   The Kingdom's blessed birth?

3. Ah, we, and we especially,
   We daughters and we sons
   Of this blest Slovak nation,
   We are the blessed ones;
   We have a special reason
   To thank God for this Gift
   And for the way he gave it
   And favored us by it.

4. While others idly waited
   To hear the holy Word
   And greeted the apostles
   With sullenness or sword,
   Our nation most sincerely
   Desired that priceless Gem,
   Invited missionaries,
   Revered and welcomed them.

5. To other people Baptism
   Came mixed with blood and force;
   Imposed and unrequested,
   They had no other course;
   But God sent us two brothers
   Of winsome friendliness,
   Methodius and Cyril,
   As saints who came to bless.

6. Elsewhere for long dark ages
   The Word was little known,
   And God was worshiped rotely
   In language not their own,
   Whereas our ancient forebears
   Heard from the very start
   In sweet maternal phrases
   The words that change the heart.

7. Imagine how our fathers
   Must have been overawed
   To read in their own language
   The mighty acts of God!
   The apostolic brothers
   So greatly loved our folk,
   They learned their tongue and gave them
   The word of life, God's Book.

8. While others boldly flaunted
   The banner of the Cross
   To plunder rights and freedom,
   And gain by others' loss,
   Our nation shared its treasure
   With meek humility,
   Rejoicing when their neighbors
   Became newborn and free.

9. Among us, pagan idols
   Fell almost by themselves,
   And in their stead grew crosses
   And churches by the twelves,
   Without the threat of murder,
   The lust of greed or gain,
   Without the tears of converts
   Who traded fear for pain.

10. Let us, like our ancestors,
    Their progeny and heirs,
    Use for our own salvation
    The means that once were theirs:
    The sacraments and Gospel,
    The Church be our concern;
    For God and for our neighbor
    Our love with fervor burn!

11. May we this true religion
    In purity preserve,
    And spread its grace and power
    In heart and life and nerve,
    Thus striving to be worthy
    To meet our pioneers
    And share with them the glory
    Of those who persevere.

7.6.7.6.D

57 COME IN HOLY AWE AND TRUTH

Come in holy awe and truth,
     Brothers, sisters, to the altar:
Children in the bloom of youth,
Elders, come with steps that falter;
All, of great or no renown,
Here, to God, we stand as one.

Those who live by cares oppressed,
Those who scamper through life gaily,
Those who know unruffled rest,
Those who weep in sorrow daily,
Friends and enemies, as one
Boldly come, approach the Throne.

By one cup and by one bread
In one body, Lord, unite us;
By the blood the Savior shed
Now with peace and joy delight us;
Reconciled with God and men,
What more cause to sing again!

By one washing, by one creed,
Each to all one Father binds us,
One the hope on which we feed,
One the grace that seeks and finds us;
Joined in love together so,
To one Table let us go.

Here ourselves we consecrate
To all truth, to love, to justice;
By this action let us state
What a holy people's trust is;
Show to all the Christ who lives,
Eat and drink the food he gives.

Tears of loneliness replace
With new tears of happy laughter,
Children of adopting grace,
See the home the world strives after:
Ours it is when we are one
With the Father and the Son.

7.8.7.8.7.7.

58   DEAR FATHER GOD, WE RISE TO SAY

Dear Father God, we rise to say,
   Your name be praised for this new day.
For health and strength our prayers we lift:
Grant every good and perfect gift.

O God the Son, we pray of you,
May all we plan and say and do
Be ever welcome in your sight,
Be done to your and our delight.

O Spirit God, preserve from fear
All those who fret and sorrow here;
And when the day of days arrives,
With fadeless glory crown our lives.

LM (8.8.8.8.)

59   GLORY BE TO YOU, O FATHER

G lory be to you, O Father,
    and thanksgiving for this food,
set before us by your mercy,
taken from your bounteous good.
Even so before us spread
your own satisfying Bread,
feed us with this heav'nly ration
that we never know starvation.

Father, who in heaven dwelling,
ever hallowed be your name;
in our hearts wield sole dominion,
may your will be all our aim.
Grant our daily bread this day,
take our wretched guilt away;
lead us not into temptation,
keep us, bring us to salvation.

8.7.8.7.7.7.8.8.

60 GOD, MY LORD, MY STRENGTH

God, my Lord, my strength, my place of hiding
And confiding
In all needs by night and day;
Though foes surround me,
And Satan marks his prey,
God shall have his way.

Christ in me, and I am freed for living
And forgiving,
Heart of flesh for lifeless stone;
Now bold to serve him,
Now cheered his love to own,
Nevermore alone.

Up, weak knees and spirit bowed in sorrow!
No tomorrow
Shall arise to beat you down;
God goes before you
And angels all around;
On your head a crown!

10.4.7.5.6.5.

G reet now the swiftly changing year
    With joy and penitence sincere.
Rejoice, rejoice, with thanks embrace
Another year of grace.

Remember now the Son of God
And how he shed his infant blood.
Rejoice, rejoice . . .

For Jesus came to wage sin's war;
This Name of names for us he bore.
Rejoice, rejoice . . .

His love abundant far exceeds
The volume of a whole year's needs.
Rejoice, rejoice . . .

With such a Lord to lead our way
In hazard or prosperity,
What need we fear in earth or space
In this new year of grace?

"All glory be to God on high,
And peace on earth!" the angels cry.
Rejoice, rejoice . . .

God, Father, Son, and Spirit, hear:
To all our pleas incline your ear;
Upon our lives rich blessings trace
In this new year of grace.

LM (8.8.8.8.)

62   HEAR ME, O MY PRECIOUS LOVE

Hear me, O my precious Love,
    When I call upon you;
Strengthen me, O Lord above,
For my trust is on you.
Loudly now my voice is crying,
Mournfully my heart is sighing:
Comfort me, comfort me, comfort me,
Worn and weary, sad and dreary.
"Return, O sinner, and love only Me,
With cross and stripe from sin I set you free;
Come repenting!

Take away all sinful fear,
Jesus, my Salvation:
For I long to have you near,
Lord, my Consolation.
Willingly I too would languish,
Follow you in cross and anguish.
Only you, only you, only you
Will I cherish lest I perish.
Ah, dearest Jesus, come, deliver me
From grief and want, I pray, and deign to be
My Sustainer.

Lord, be merciful, I pray,
Pardon my transgression!
Let my soul no longer stray;
Make it your possession.
On the cross your bitter torment
Wrought my dying soul's restorement,
So that I, even I, even I,
By your merit life inherit.
Ah, dearest Jesus, come and bear me up
Above these agonies: remove my cup!
Lord, have mercy!

Irregular   Copyright © 1987 by Jaroslav J. Vajda

63 HOW LOVELY AND HOW PLEASANT

H ow lovely and how pleasant
    When people dwell in peace
And love is ever present
To bind them each to each,
And love is ever present
To bind them each to each.

As dew upon the mountain
Refreshes every flower,
So love springs like a fountain
For those who know its power,
So love springs like a fountain
For those who know its power.

Like sweetest oil pervading
This temple where we meet,
So flows a joy unfading
O'er those at Jesus' feet,
So flows a joy unfading
O'er those at Jesus' feet.

7.6.7.6.7.6.

64 LET OUR GLADNESS BANISH SADNESS

Let our gladness banish sadness all throughout creation!
    God, whose favor sent our Savior, praise with adoration!
He is born in a stall,
Now he lies, Infant small,
In a manger, heavenly Stranger, Lord of all, Lord of all.

Whom the sages and the ages anxiously awaited,
Angels proudly herald loudly in their songs elated.
Let us, too, in these days,
Thankful hearts gladly raise;
To the tender Infant render all our praise, all our praise.

Child appealing, Light revealing, Jesus Christ, our Pleasure;
God, yet very Son of Mary, Heaven's Gift and Treasure.
Mighty King, gentle Friend,
As our Lord to us bend,
With your blessing us caressing, now descend, now descend.

14.14.6.6.14.

65   MAKE SONGS OF JOY

Make songs of joy to Christ our head, Alleluia!
He lives again who once was dead! Alleluia!

Our life was purchased by his loss, Alleluia!
He died our death upon the cross. Alleluia!

O death, where is your deadly sting? Alleluia!
Assumed by our triumphant King! Alleluia!

And where your victory, O grave, Alleluia!
When one like Christ has come to save? Alleluia!

Behold, the tyrants, one and all, Alleluia!
Before our mighty Savior fall! Alleluia!

For this be praised the Son who rose, Alleluia!
The Father and the Holy Ghost! Alleluia!

8.4.8.4.

66 YOUR HEART, O GOD, IS GRIEVED

Cantor: O God, Father in heaven, have mercy upon us.

Your heart, O God, is grieved, we know,
By every evil, every woe;
Upon your cross-forsaken Son
Our death is laid, our peace is won.

Cantor: O Son of God, Redeemer of the world, have mercy upon us.

Your arms extend, O Christ, to save
From sting of death and grasp of grave;
Your scars before the Father move
His heart to mercy at such love.

Cantor: O God, Holy Spirit, have mercy upon us.

O lavish Giver, come to aid
The children that your word has made.
Now make us grow and help us pray;
Bring joy and comfort, come to stay.

LM and Chant

Slovak Carols and Songs

Slovak Carols and Songs

Having known a number of Slovakian Christmas carols from early childhood, I was nevertheless surprised to discover that my ancestors' small homeland had produced hundreds, if not thousands, of Christmas carols and shepherd songs during its 1100-year history as a Christian nation. The impetus for translating some of them came from Joseph Duris, a Roman Catholic 1948 refugee from Slovakia, who was separated from his wife and children in a 35-year exile in Cleveland, Ohio, where he served as organist and choir director. He approached me in 1955 with a request to translate twelve Christmas carols and a peasant stroller's play for a symposium entitled *Slovak Christmas*, to be published by the Slovak Institute of Cleveland, Ohio, and Rome, Italy, in 1960. These carols were set for various voice groupings by several arrangers and have achieved a fairly wide circulation in the book as well as in sheet music form. In their land of origin, these charming songs have been banned from publication in choral arrangements as well as in recordings, so it may be that their survival may depend on their publication in English translation until their "Egyptian exile" ends as did the Flight of their Subject until Herod left the scene.

A special type of dilemma faces the translator of Christmas carols and songs, whose imagery is repeated in endless variations and where the memory of a certain carol is triggered by its familiar melody. In most cases the translator has to decide between rendering a fairly close approximation of the original, which will also be repetitious, or strike out toward pictures and phrases that acquire a freshness by their departure from the original. Most of the following translations opt for the former choice.

Slight revisions have been made in this publication of the texts from their original appearance in English, and the few traces of Mariolatry in some of the originals have been amended for the sake of wider ecumenical usage without making their theology unacceptable to Catholic singers.

67 A CUCKOO FLEW OUT OF THE WOOD

A cuckoo flew out of the wood, cuckoo, cuckoo,
Atwitter in holiday mood, cuckoo, cuckoo;
There at the manger, perched on the hay,
Greeting the Stranger born on this day:
Cuckoo, cuckoo, cuckoo . . .

And, leaving his sheep all behind, cuckoo, cuckoo,
A shepherd the Savior would find, cuckoo, cuckoo;
Singing with joy there with all the rest
To the new Boy there in his crude nest:
Cuckoo, cuckoo, cuckoo . . .

Now hear the sweet bells as they ring: ding, dong . . .
In chorus with nature now sing: ding, dong . . .
Angels and bird there, shepherd and we,
Let all be heard there in symphony:
Ding, dong, ding, dong, ding, dong . . .

12.12.9.9.12.

68 CHRISTIANS, GATHER ROUND

C hristians, gather round,
⠀⠀Hear the joyful sound!
Christians, gather round,
Hear the joyful sound!
Man by God this night befriended,
Heaven's light to earth descended.
Christians, gather round,
Hear the joyful sound!

Hear we now a voice
Bidding us rejoice.
Hear we now a voice
Bidding us rejoice.
He who in the Godhead rested
Now in flesh is manifested.
Hear we now a voice
Bidding us rejoice.

Glory pure and bright
Breaks upon our night.
Glory pure and bright
Breaks upon our night.
See our fields with splendor blazing,
And our hills in light amazing!
Christians, gather round,
Hear the joyful sound!

5.5.5.5.8.8.5.5.

69 COME NOW, SHEPHERDS, QUICKLY COME

C ome now, shepherds, quickly come to Bethl'em's manger lowly,
    There for you and for the world is born the Christ Child holy.
At this rare and royal meeting
Sing a song of joyful greeting:
Welcome, King of heaven,
Welcome to the earth!

Born immaculate, the Son of Mary, virgin maiden,
See the manger crude and cold with bread from heaven laden.
Whom the prophets died proclaiming,
She this very night is naming,
Jesus Christ our Savior
Now for us is born!

Blest Redeemer, precious Flower, wonderful Lord Jesus,
Prince of Peace, almighty Savior, from our sins release us!
King of heaven, Lord supernal,
Take us to our home eternal.
O beloved Jesus,
Grant us what we pray!

14.14.8.8.6.5.

70 DEAR LITTLE JESUS, WE COME TO THY BED

Dear little Jesus, we come to Thy bed,
  Nothing we seek but to be comforted.
Thee we would fondle,
Thee we would cradle,
Thy tender glory around us spread.
Slumber on sweetly now, precious One,
Heavenly Infant, our God's only Son!

Dream, softly dream, Thou blest Flower divine,
Lord of the heavens, asleep in this shrine.
Angels acclaim Thee,
Our God we name Thee,
Born of a Virgin to set us free.
Slumber on sweetly now, precious One,
Heavenly Infant, our God's only Son!

Slumber, Thou Treasure of fabulous worth,
Soft be the straw-bed of Thy lowly birth.
Bring us salvation
And consolation,
Grant us Thy blessing while ages run.
Slumber on sweetly now, precious One,
Heavenly Infant, our God's only Son!

10.10.5.5.9.9.10.

71 HEAVEN'S DAWN IS BREAKING BRIGHTLY

Heaven's dawn is breaking brightly, happy Christmas morn!
Of the blessed Virgin Mary Jesus Christ is born.

Chorus:

To Him let us sing, praise and honor bring;
O Thou precious, tender Infant, to Thy name we sing;
O Thou precious, tender Infant, to Thy name we sing!

Hear the angel song proclaiming: "Peace to all the earth!
Have no fear, I bring you tidings of your Savior's birth!"

Chorus:

13.13.5.5.13.13.

72 LO, OUR SHEPHERD IN A MANGER

L o, our Shepherd in a manger,
  Born to save his sheep from danger,
To small Bethlehem he came.
Alleluia, alleluia, bless his name!

For a single sheep departed
From his fold, he, broken-hearted,
Searches till he brings it home;
For but one he leaves the ninety-nine alone.

8.8.7.11.

73 LO, WHAT A WONDER

L o, what a wonder fills all the world with joy,
    Mary, the Virgin poor, bears a baby Boy,
Son of the living God, Lord of the earth,
Blesses poor Bethlehem with his glad birth.

Softly the Mother rocks Jesus in her arm,
Singing this lullaby of such tender charm:
"Sleep, little Child of mine, peacefully rest,
Of your poor swaddling clothes make you a nest."

11.11.10.10.

74 OH, WHAT TIDINGS BRIGHT

Oh, what tidings bright come to us tonight!
    Oh, what tidings bright come to us tonight!
Light of light to us descending,
God himself our gloom is ending,
Oh, what tidings bright come to us tonight!

Hear we now a voice bidding us rejoice.
Hear we now a voice bidding us rejoice.
He who in the Godhead rested
Now in flesh is manifested,
To redeem us all from the devil's thrall!

Glory pure and bright breaks upon our night.
Glory pure and bright breaks upon our night.
See the fields aglow and blazing
And the hills in light amazing!
Oh, what tidings bright come to us tonight!

10.10.8.8.10.

75 OUT OF THE FOREST A CUCKOO FLEW

Out of the forest a cuckoo flew, cuckoo!
   Down to the manger her Lord to view, cuckoo!
And there she honors him as she sings
Her praises to the King of kings.
Cuckoo, cuckoo, cuckoo!

There sits a dove on a little tree, curroo!
Adding his song to the harmony, curroo!
He wants to show, this happiest morn,
His thankful heart that Jesus is born.
Curroo, curroo, curroo!

11.11.9.9.(8).6.

Out to the hills, to the forest run,
    What is that burning there like the sun?
Joy supernal's there appearing,
None has ever been so cheering.
Run, shepherds, run to the stable mean,
Then come and tell us what you have seen.

"There a young Virgin has borne a Child,
There in a manger he lies so mild,
Our Messiah long awaited,
Born a man, yet uncreated;
Come, let us worship our noble Lord,
Add yet our voice to the angel chord!"

O Son of God, sent from heav'n above,
Grant us poor sinners your gracious love,
That we may extol you ever,
Praise and worship you, dear Savior;
Come, O Redeemer, and with us dwell,
Bless us, beloved Immanuel!

9.9.8.8.9.9.

77   RISE UP, BETHL'EM SHEPHERDS, RISE

R ise up, Bethl'em shepherds, rise!
     Lift your eyes up to the skies!
Listen to the word
No one's ear has heard:
"There is born to us a Savior,
God's own Son with heav'nly favor;
Let us go and greet
Him with praises meet!

Gifts we give he will receive
On this happy Christmas Eve
From our hearts of love
Kindled from above.
He will hear the prayers we send him,
Grant them, and to us will bend him,
That we all may share
His own glory there.

7.7.5.5.8.8.5.5.

78 SHEPHERDS ALL, COME

Shepherds all, come, and give ear to our song!
  Shepherds all, come, for the Savior is born!
See what this very day we are given:
Our one Redeemer sent down from heaven.
Glory to God!

Shepherds all, come, and abandon your sheep,
Go to the stable, your Savior to seek;
There in a manger lies Christ anointed,
Whom as our Savior God has appointed.
Glory to God!

Now join the shepherds, to Bethlehem go,
That we like them God's redemption may know;
Here is the Word made flesh, bow before him,
He dwells among us, let us adore him.
Come and adore him, the Savior of all.

10.10.10.10.4.(10)

79 SHEPHERDS OF BETHLEHEM

S hepherds of Bethlehem,
    Come, see the diadem
Sparkling brightly in the heavens high;
Out of that blinding glow
To all who dwell below
Angels shout their very happy cry:
Lo, a poor maiden bore a pure Baby
And laid him down in a cradle of hay,
And laid him down in a cradle of hay.

Angels declare to us
Tidings most glorious:
Christ the Lord has left his throne above,
Now to our race descends
And to our nature bends,
God and man in one to show his love.
Lo, a poor maiden bore a pure Baby
And laid him down in a cradle of hay,
And laid him down in a cradle of hay.

"O precious Floweret
In your crude bassinet,
Bless and keep our valleys and our fields,
That we may honor you
And render service due
With the bounty that our pasture yields."
Lo, a poor maiden bore a pure Baby
And laid him down in a cradle of hay,
And laid him down in a cradle of hay.

6.6.9.6.6.9.5.5.10.10.

Slumber, lovely Baby,
    May the rough crib hay be
Soft beneath you, newborn Boy,
Jesus, gift of purest joy.
We will rock you soothingly
That your sleep may smoother be.
Jesus, our dear Jesus,
Dream a dream that eases
Your fond mother's pain,
Your fond mother's pain.

Meadow, farm and mountain,
Rippling stream and fountain,
Welcome him with gifts and flow'rs
To this lovely land of ours,
To the song of winging birds
We will add our joyful words,
Join the whole creation
In our adoration,
With our glad refrain,
With our glad refrain.

Woods, now calm your noises,
Still your whispered voices,
Let the Infant have his sleep,
Resting where the straw be deep;
And the roses burning red
Send soft fragrance to his bed.
Quiet, lambs, the Baby
Sleeping here so gravely
Will forever reign,
Will forever reign.

6.6.7.7.7.7.6.6.5.5.

81   TELL US, SHEPHERDS, WHY SO JOYFUL

Tell us, shepherds, why so joyful, what was it you saw?
  What was it that made you tremble, made you run for awe?
"We saw a little Child,
Wondrous and, oh, so mild,
Born in Bethlehem this night."

How is it that no one heard this, none but you alone?
I would have gone with you gladly, had I only known.
"Angels proclaimed the Word,
Theirs was the voice we heard,
That our Savior Christ was born."

Reach to us, O little Jesus, reach your little hand,
In your infant arms enfold the souls of every land.
Here make your welcome home,
To all your servants come,
Blest Redeemer whom we love!

13.13.6.6.7.

82 WAKE TO THE WONDER

Wake to the wonder appearing above
    God has created for us out of love!
Never before has the world been so visited,
Never before has the world been so visited,
Never before have we seen such a sight
Filling the heaven and earth with its light.

Shepherds, be calm, you have nothing to fear;
I bring you tidings of comfort and cheer.
I am a messenger sent from the throne of God,
I am a messenger sent from the throne of God,
I come to you with his very own word:
Go, see in Bethlehem Jesus your Lord!

What you have waited for God to you brings;
Go there and you will find the King of kings:
Jesus, an infant, yet Ruler of rulers he,
Jesus, an infant, yet Ruler of rulers he,
There in a manger on hay in a stall
Lies your Redeemer, the Savior of all!

10.10.12.12.10.10.

83   WAKE UP, BROTHER, LISTEN

Wake up, brother, listen to the wondrous news,
    What at midnight startled all our lambs and ewes.
They had just come in from grazing
And lay down when the amazing light appeared,
And a sound from heaven woke them, strange and feared.

Come to Bethl'em, come now, to the blessed site,
We shall see what happened there this very night.
Just to spend a little while there,
And to see the precious Child there, in the hay,
Wrapped in swaddling garments, as the angels say.

11.11.8.11.11.

While Mary rocks her child to rest,
    Crying and wakeful at her breast,
Soothing him, softly shuts his eyes
And sings to him sweet lullabies:
"O precious, so lovely, O Jesu mine!
O precious, so lovely, O Jesu mine!

"You are my sweetness, made of flesh,
You are my gladness, high and fresh,
Sleep, tender Rose, and warm my heart;
With all my love I gave you birth:
O precious, so lovely, O Jesu mine!
O precious, so lovely, O Jesu mine!

"Of mighty rulers you are King,
All that we need your love will bring,
Here on the straw so weak, so small,
You are the Savior, Lord of all:
O precious, so lovely, O Jesu mine!
O precious, so lovely, O Jesu mine!"

8.8.8.8.10.10.

German Hymns

85   ALL WHO CRAVE A GREATER MEASURE

All who crave a greater measure
   Of this blessed Christmas pleasure,
Loo-la, loo-la, loo-la, . . .
Pause and hear the Virgin mother
Sing to sleep our heavenly Brother,
God's and her beloved Son:
"Loo-la, loo-la, loo-la, . . .
Softly, softly slumber, Jesus, dearest Child."

"Take the brightest flowers of morning,
Garlands for your crib's adorning,
Loo-la, loo-la, loo-la, . . .
Sleep, my Joy, who would not choose you,
Sleep, my Hope, I dare not lose you,
Sleep, my true, my heavenly Bread.
Loo-la, loo-la, loo-la, . . .
Softly, softly slumber, Savior of the world."

8.8.8.8.8.8.7.8.8.11.

86 BREAK FORTH IN PRAISE TO GOD

Break forth in praise to God,
 You cheerful cherubim;
To yours our voices add,
You shining seraphim.
With reverence discreet
Your feet and faces cover;
To taste of joy so sweet
From God, our heav'nly Lover,
Unite our earthly tongues
With your celestial songs:
Holy, holy, holy, Lord God of Sabaoth,
You are the most high God,
Lofty, sublime, and holy,
Lofty, sublime, and holy.

Before your majesty
We join the heav'nly throng
To stand before your throne
And share their endless song.
Eternal Three-in-One,
We view with awe and wonder,
O bright angelic Sun,
O undiminished Splendor,
We glorify, adore,
And praise you evermore:
Holy, holy, holy, Lord God of Sabaoth,
You are the God of might,
To you we sing thrice "Holy!"
To you we sing thrice "Holy!"

The Father now we laud,
The Maker of all things;
The Savior, Son of God,
Most worthy King of kings;
And Holy Spirit, you,
Your children gently feeding,
As you have made us new,
To our salvation leading,
So by the faith you give,
May we in glory live.
Joyful, joyful, joyful, are all who dwell with you,
O blessed Trinity,
You free us from all sorrow,
You free us from all sorrow.

6.6.6.6.6.7.6.7.6.6. Refrain

Copyright © 1980 by Jaroslav J. Vajda

87 DEAREST LORD JESUS, WHY ARE YOU DELAYING

Dearest Lord Jesus, why are you delaying?
    Come, see what burdens my soul are dismaying;
Come now and take me wherever you will,
Save me, oh, save me; your promise fulfill!
Dearest Lord Jesus, why are you delaying?
Come, see what burdens my soul are dismaying.

It is enough, Lord, so come and deliver
Body and soul from evil forever.
Come now, my fading assurance renew,
All that I am I surrender to you.
Come, see what burdens my soul are dismaying,
Come, as you promised, no longer delaying.

Irregular   Copyright © 1987 by Jaroslav J. Vajda

88   FOR YOUR MERCY I IMPLORE YOU

For your mercy I implore you,
    Father, hear my fearful cry;
As your child I come before you,
Light my pathway lest I die.
Stop the foes who mock and hound me,
Save me from their deadly harm;
When your love and might surround me,
I rest safely in your arm.

8.7.8.7.D.

89 HEAR ME, HELP ME, GRACIOUS SAVIOR

Hear me, help me, gracious Savior,
    Turn in mercy, I implore;
Should you mark sins, I could never
Stand before you evermore.

Shall my sorrow last forever,
Shall my enemies rejoice?
Weak and helpless, O my Savior,
I await your soothing voice.

8.7.8.7.

90   IF GOD IS ABSENT, ALL THE COST

If God is absent, all the cost
 And pains that build the house are lost;
If God the city does not keep,
The watchful guards as well may sleep.

In vain you rise before the sun,
Still hungry when your work is done;
The bread you fret about is found,
When you awake, upon the ground.

The Lord, whose love for all we share
Makes every child of ours his heir,
And in his strong protective hand
The young he blesses safely stand.

How blest the parents, who to heaven
Devote the children God has given;
No shame or scandal shall they know
As God protects them from the Foe.

To God the Father and the Son
And Holy Spirit on one throne,
Whom saints here and above adore,
Be glory now and evermore.

LM (8.8.8.8.)

91   LORD, WE HOLD YOUR GOODNESS PRECIOUS

L ord, we hold your goodness precious,
   In it we are most secure;
We shall sing, for love so gracious,
Joyful anthems evermore.

8.7.8.7.

92 NOW SHINE, BRIGHT GLOW OF MAJESTY

Now shine, bright glow of majesty
Your long-prepared epiphany;
Our way lit by your burning,
To you we are returning,
Our journey through this earthly night
Immersed in your baptismal light.
O highest, holy Jesus Christ,
Never will you forsake us;
You are the Sun that feeds our lives;
By your strong hand now take us
And lead us from this gloomy thrall
Into your royal banquet hall,
Where we shall see you All-in-All.

Irregular

93   O FATHER, SEND THE SPIRIT DOWN

O Father, send the Spirit down,
   The Gift of gifts we most would own,
Upon your dear Son's prompting.
We pray, as we were taught by him,
Our cup of joy fill to the brim,
And never leave us wanting.

No one in all the world can claim
This noble Gift by force or fame;
We have no power to gain it.
Here nothing counts but love and grace,
And God's acceptance of the price:
Christ's life and cross obtain it.

8.8.7.8.8.7.

94 O JOYOUS CHRISTMAS NIGHT

O joyous Christmas Night,
        None in all time so cheering,
Wherein the heav'nly Sun,
Our Christ makes his appearing!
Bright gleam of Jacob's Star,
Sweet, happy, hopeful Ray,
Come, pierce the whole wide world
With light this beauteous Day!

All Christians now rejoice,
Fresh hope your terrors stilling,
For God has kept his word,
His promises fulfilling;
True to his loving pledge
He sends his bodied Word
For us to see and hold,
Our gracious God's Reward.

The world is blest today
With this most holy Savior,
A gift of such vast worth
We stammer at his favor;
Our praises will not make
Him richer than He is,
But he enriches us
With his eternal bliss.

6.7.6.7.6.6.6.6.

The rescue we were waiting for
  Has come most undeservedly,
While we were groping on the floor
Of deep despair, what did we see?
The hand of Jesus, God's own Son,
Came reaching down to us alone:
No one but he could save us.

Chained by the law and its demands
And crippled by the curse of sin,
All offerings smeared by guilty hands,
The walls of hopelessness closed in,
While in the mirror all I saw
Was weakling, rebel, fatal flaw —
And found no one to save me.

The law, I found, was not the way
To life and health, to joy and peace;
I'd piled up debts I could not pay,
From death there was no sure release.
And then, when in the deepest throes
Of gloom, I heard the hammer blows
Constructing my salvation.

The gift I had no right to claim,
A life to compensate my loss,
By grace from God the Father came:
My Substitute upon my cross.
My pardon there was read to me,
Beneath that God-forsaken tree —
And I am free forever!

Secure within his warm embrace,
Join in the Savior's freedom song:
Show Christ to every downcast face,
Shout Christ to all the dying throng!
Sing loving Father, gracious Son,
Sing living Spirit, freedom won,
For now and through all ages!

8.8.8.8.D

96 WHAT LOVE, LORD JESUS, THAT YOU GO

What love, Lord Jesus, that you go
  So willingly to offer
Yourself for me, a sinner who
Has caused what you must suffer.
Let me at least, my Great High Priest,
Walk in your footsteps weeping;
My tears shall flow with cries of woe,
Watch o'er your sorrows keeping.

'Tis I, Lord Jesus, I confess,
Who should have borne sin's wages
And lost the peace of heavenly bliss
Through everlasting ages.
Instead I hear you volunteer;
My punishment you carry.
Your death and blood lead me to God,
Where I by grace may tarry.

Lord Jesus, for such love divine
What can I find to render?
There is no treasure I call mine
That I would not surrender:
Myself alone, and all I own,
In love to serve before you;
And then at last, when time is past,
In heaven I shall adore you.

8.7.8.7.4.4.7.4.4.7.

97 WORLD, FOR ALL YOUR GAIN AND PLEASURE

World, for all your gain and pleasure,
    Your horizons gleaming bright,
I desire the lasting treasure
As I face the coming night.
Death, I know, must end this strife,
Life will once give way to Life;
All the best is yet to be,
Peace and joy eternally.

When I know such life awaits me,
I can live more freely here;
Christ, my guide and hope, supports me,
Fills my days on earth with cheer.
Here I see his work begun,
In his rising victory won.
But the best is yet to be:
Life with him eternally.

8.7.8.7.7.7.7.7.

German Carols and Anthems

German Carols and Anthems

Some of the remarks concerning the procedure followed in translating Slovak carols and songs apply to the following renditions of a number of German carols and anthems. Most of these English texts originated in requests for English texts for choral settings by Hermann Schroeder in a series produced by Concordia Publishing House.

98 A DOVE FLEW DOWN FROM HEAVEN

A dove flew down from heaven,
      A dove rare and pure,
In angel garb appearing,
To greet a maid demure:
"All grace I bring you,
Tender, lovely maid,
No soul with such adorning
Has ever been arrayed."
Mercy, Lord, have mercy.

"I bring you joyous greetings:
The Lord is with you!
A Child you will be bearing;
You must believe it's true.
So welcome, welcome,
Open wide your heart,
That God upon this visit
His favor may impart."
Mercy, Lord, have mercy.

To this the Virgin bowing,
Responded with awe:
"If this is what He wishes,
His wish shall be my law.
Yet more than willing
I surrender me,
If such Love is my Master,
His servant I will be."
Mercy, Lord, have mercy.

And so the Gift was given,
Our Helper in need,
New Life to dwell among us,
Eternal God indeed!
This Jesus Christ-Child,
Son whom Mary bore,
Is come to be our Savior,
To heaven our open Door.
Mercy, Lord, have mercy.

7.5.7.6.5.5.6.6.6.

99   DELICATE CHILD OF ROYAL LINE

D elicate Child of royal line,
　　Now take your rest and slumber.
Sheep in the meadow lately fed
Share in your peace and slumber.
　　Close your eyes tight,
　　Calm is the night,
Slumber, my dear One, slumber.

Brightest of angels trail your train,
Row upon endless number,
Filling the sky with bursting joy,
Trumpets and harps and drummers.
　　Close your eyes tight,
　　Safe in their light
Slumber, my dear One, slumber.

8.7.8.7.4.4.7.

100 IN BETHLEHEM A WONDER

In Bethlehem a wonder
  Is born a Child for me;
And when this Gift I ponder,
His own I wish to be.
Ah, yes, ah, yes, his own I wish to be.

O little Child, be to me
More precious than before,
In happy times or gloomy
I wish to love you more.
Ah, yes, ah, yes, I wish to love you more.

True God, I now discover
You in my flesh and blood;
Gladly I bind me over
To you, my highest Good.
Ah, yes, ah, yes, to you, my highest Good.

7.6.7.6.10.

N ow to this Babe so tender,
  Now to this Babe so tender,
Your heart in love surrender,
In spirit gladly take him
Up in your arms and rock him:
O Jesus, O Jesus so sweet,
O Jesus so sweet.

Bend to the Baby singing,
Bend to the Baby singing,
Your offerings to him bringing,
Come, show how you adore him,
Lift laud and praise before him:
O Jesus, O Jesus so sweet,
O Jesus so sweet.

His hands and feet caressing,
His hands and feet caressing,
His heart, too, greet in blessing,
In humble awe come near him,
As God and Word revere him:
O Jesus, O Jesus so sweet,
O Jesus so sweet.

Now spend your life in serving,
Now spend your life in serving
This Gift beyond deserving,
Until with angels sharing
You wear the crown he's wearing.
O Jesus, O Jesus so sweet,
O Jesus so sweet.

7.7.7.7.7.8.5.

S leep softly, softly, beautiful Jesus,
   Sleep softly, darling Child,
You close your eyes, the whole world sleeps,
All night the heavenly Father keeps,
Keeps watch for us, for us,
Keeps watch for us, for us.

See Mary and Joseph standing nearby
While still the cattle lie,
Soon will the shepherds running come
To see the wonder of Bethlehem,
To marvel and adore,
To marvel and adore.

10.6.8.8.6.6.

S leep well, dear heavenly Boy, sleep well,
    In slumber take your rest.
Soft angel wings, Immanuel,
Will fan you in your nest;
And we poor shepherds, kneeling here,
Sing you our lullaby sincere:
    Slumber, slumber,
    Rest in peaceful slumber.

Around you Mary folds her care
To watch the nighttime through,
And Joseph dares not stir the air
Lest he awaken you;
The little sheep in barn and stall
Before the Infant silent fall,
    Slumber, slumber,
    Rest in peaceful slumber.

The rage of those you've come to save
Will take your life one day,
And lay you in an early grave —
So rest you while you may.
Poor Child of heaven, your eyelids close
And spend this night in sweet repose.
    Slumber, slumber,
    Rest in peaceful slumber.

8.6.8.6.8.8.4.6.

104   UP, O SHEPHERDS

U p, O shepherds, up from sleep,
    Break your slumber's fastening.
For a time forsake your sheep,
To the manger hastening.
Sing now: "What a blessed night,
Bringing us salvation's light,
For to us from heaven's throne
Comes the Father's only Son!"

Shepherds, just go bravely in,
There's no cause for terror.
Comfort, grace, and peace within —
Never were they nearer.
At this cradle, come to view
How the Savior welcomes you.
See his heart with love afire:
Do not spurn this Babe's desire.

Precious little Child divine,
Yet the Lord's anointed:
Though we be so few and plain,
Don't be disappointed.
Please receive our homage true,
Son of God, we worship you.
Brighter shine these stars and moon
Than the sun at height of noon.

7.6.7.6.7.7.7.7.

Wake, shepherds, awake,
    Your sadness forsake.
Bright angels are swinging
From heaven and singing:
    "Your joy is now near,
    The Savior is here!"

Come, shepherds, in haste
To Someone so chaste:
With flutes fill his heart full
Of songs gay and artful;
    Come, find in a stall
    The Savior of all.

They came and they heard
The wonderful word,
Then told one another
Of Jesus, their Brother,
    And everyone found
    A King to be crowned.

They greeted with joy
This heavenly Boy
In wonder amazing,
In carols and praising.
    Their pipes echo still
    At night on the hill.

5.5.6.6.5.5.

Hungarian Hymns

106 BLESSED BE THE PRECIOUS BABY

Blessed be the precious Baby,
newborn Prince in Bethl'em's stable!
Welcome we the Gift God gave us;
who but he was born to save us?

See the Morning Star arising!
Who can sleep through such surprising?
Hear the happy breezes bringing
news the angel choirs are singing.

Celebrate this Evening holy,
everyone, both great and lowly:
gift from heaven meant to please us,
birthday of our Savior, Jesus!

LM (8.8.8.8.) Trochaic

FROM THE SHADOW OF MY PAIN

From the shadow of my pain,
    from the shadow of my pain,
unto you, my God, I cry:
hear my fervent prayer,
let me not despair,
nor be swallowed by my sorrows
in this prison where I sigh.

No one seeks to do me harm,
no one seeks to do me harm,
but my enemy is me
and your judgment dread
breaking on my head.
There's no hiding from your chiding;
save my soul from jeopardy.

Lord, I beg you, crush my pride,
Lord, I beg you, crush my pride,
give me true repentance, please!
Something in me cries:
let me realize
how I hurt you and desert you!
What will bring me to my knees!

I am wracked by endless sobs,
I am wracked by endless sobs,
yet my weeping brings no tears.
Morning, noon, and night,
Satan lies in wait,
and resisting his persisting,
I am slain by my own fears.

Let your holy will be done,
Let your holy will be done;
I surrender to your rod
if someone may gain
from my grief and pain.
Ah, but rather, like a father,
save me still, my gracious God!

7.7.7.5.5.8.7.

Who's that sitting on the ground,
    center of a motley crowd?
Did you see him looking at us,
hear his gentle words?

Says a gruff man with a frown:
"Go away, you little ones!
Children cannot understand him;
he is God's own Son!"

Ah, but we do understand,
and we love that kindly man.
Can't we offer little praises
if a songbird can?

Listen to the Master say:
"I will not turn you away;
more than birds, you make me happy
when I hear you pray."

7.7.8.5.

BACKGROUND NOTES ON
HYMNS AND CAROLS

1   A COMET BLAZED ACROSS THE SKIES   LM (8.8.8.8.)

Based on	Revelation 14:6, 7
Theme	Commemoration of Martin Luther's birth
Written	1 July 1982
Suggested tune	*ERHALT UNS, HERR*

In view of the approaching 400th anniversary observance of Martin Luther's birth in 1983, I wrote this commemorative hymn without an assignment. It was meant to illustrate Rev. 14:6, 7, traditionally held by Lutherans to be a prophecy of the Reformer. To connect the text subliminally with Luther and his hymn, *Erhalt uns, Herr, bei deinem Wort*, it was written with that tune in mind. Line 5:1 is taken word for word from Catherine Winkworth's translation of line 2:1 of Nikolaus Selnecker's hymn on the preservation of the Word and the Church, *Ach, bleib bei uns, Herr Jesu Christ* (*The Lutheran Hymnal*, 292). Selnecker was one of the great champions of Lutheran orthodoxy and one of the framers of the unifying *Formula of Concord*, 1577. To my knowledge this hymn was not used in the commemoration, though it may be appropriate for commemorating the Reformer's birth on or near November 10.

2   AMID THE WORLD'S BLEAK WILDERNESS   Irregular

Based on	John 15:1-8
Theme	Faith, Witness, Union with Christ Hymn of the Day, Easter V (B)
Written	19 December 1975
Suggested tune	*GRANTON* by Richard W. Hillert

This hymn was written at the suggestion of the sainted E. Theo DeLaney, who indicated a need for a hymn on the subject of the Vine and the Branches as a hymn of the day for the Fifth Sunday of Easter in the *Lutheran Book of Worship* then being prepared.

In studying the various Scriptural references to this subject, I thought of having the verse form of the hymn resemble a grape vine. It occurred to me that the classic form of the *terza rima*, which Dante used in the Divine Comedy, by its definition depicts the interwoven nature of a vine; "a verse form consisting of tercets usually in iambic pentameter with an interlaced rhyme scheme (as aba, bcb, cdc, etc.) in English poetry." I took the liberty of rendering the verses in quadrameter along the lines of such familiar three-line stanza hymns as *O filii et filiae*. I had hoped that the composer of the melody for the text would try to reflect the interwoven nature of the text by using a rhythm similar to that of *O filii et filiae*, in a major key and allowing for the repetition of lines one and two as the tune for the last stanza, which is a sort of refrain. Visually and melodically, the hymn was to resemble a vine and its branches. Richard W. Hillert's tune *GRANTON* succeeded in expressing this intention.

Leslie Brandt, the writer of *Psalms/Now* and other devotional books in that series, was inspired to write *Meditations along the Journey of Faith* (Concordia, 1986) on the basis of this hymn text.

Publications: (See Appendix 1)
                   Lutheran Book of Worship, 1978
                   Lutheran Worship, 1982
                   Hymnal Supplement II, 1987

3   BEFORE THE MARVEL OF THIS NIGHT   8.8.8.8.8.8.8.6.

Based on   Luke 2:13, 14
Theme   Christmas/The angels' song
Written   1 January 1979
Suggested tune   *MARVEL* by Carl Schalk

In response to a request for a Christmas or Epiphany song from the editors of *CHRISTMAS*: An American Annual of Christmas Literature and Art, for their 1981 edition, this was one of five Christmas songs chosen for publication. One of the suggested themes was the angel song. But what could one possibly say in music that had not already been covered in the hundreds of extant Christmas carols and songs? I decided to conjecture how the angel hosts may have prepared and rehearsed that first Christmas song with a handful of shepherds as their audience? Projecting my experience in choir singing and conducting to that divine chorus, I wrote the text for which Carl Schalk composed a new melody, since it was not intended for any existing meter. Subsequently this song has enjoyed wide popularity and usage in Schalk's choir arrangement published by Augsburg Publishing House.

Publications: "Angel Song in *Christmas*, 1981   (See Appendix 2)
                   Before the Marvel of this Night, 1982
                       (See Appendix 3-A)
                   Hymnal Supplement II, 1987   (See Appendix 1)

4 BEFORE YOUR AWESOME MAJESTY   LM (8.8.8.8.)

Based on	Psalm 93
Theme	Adoration/Praise
Written	12 October 1985
Suggested tune	*DER HERR IST KÖNIG HERRLICH SCHÖN*

Alphabetically listed, this is the first of eight Becker Psalter texts prepared for the 15th Annual Bach Cantata Series presented at Grace Lutheran Church, River Forest, Illinois, 1985-86. The Cantata Series committee selected eight versified Psalms (23, 30, 46, 93, 103, 104, 111, and 130) from the Cornelius Backer Psalter of 1602 in their Heinrich Schuetz (1628) choral settings and asked for a new set of psalm paraphrases to fit the particular chorales.

The following texts were prepared for the series in contemporary language and imagery and to give them a New Testament application by unfolding the fulfillment concealed in their Old Testament version. The meter and rhyme schemes were suggested by the German texts for which the Heinrich Schuetz settings were made, though the English texts, while based on the Biblical Psalms, are not translations of the German texts, but are original paraphrases/hymns.

This background commentary applies to all eight "Becker Psalter" texts:

Before your awesome majesty (Psalm 93)
Count your blessings, O my soul (Psalm 104)
Give glory, all creation (Psalm 103)
I praise you, Lord, in every hour (Psalm 30)
In hopelessness and near despair (Psalm 130)
Lord, I must praise you (Psalm 111)
Though mountains quake and oceans roar (Psalm 46)
You, Jesus, are my shepherd true (Psalm 23)

Publications: *Eight Psalms*, 1987   (See Appendix 2)

5 BEGIN THE SONG OF GLORY NOW   LMD (8.8.8.8.8.8.8.8.)

Based on	1 Corinthians 15
Theme	Easter/Resurrection/Music/Praise
Written	21 April 1985

Prompted by a search by the Hymn Society of America for hymns on the theme of music, this Easter hymn attempts to tie the ultimate reason for singing to the key event in history and our faith-life: the Resurrection.

"If Christ is not risen, your faith is futile; you are still in your sins" and hence without any reason for singing. "But now Christ is risen from the dead," and we indeed have reason to revel in his victory with shouts of triumph, with music and praise, like the Resurrexit in Bach's *B-Minor Mass*. Another clue from Bach's dedication of his music is referred to in 3:5, 6, his superscription "INJ" and his postscript, "SDG." The composition of this hymn was inspired also by the tercentennary celebration of Bach's birth in 1985.

6 CATCH THE VISION! SHARE THE GLORY!   9.9.8.8.9.8.9.

Based on	Matthew 28:18-20; Acts 1:8
Theme	Church/Mission/Evangelism/Witness
Written	26 February 1986
Suggested tune	*VISION* by Carl Schalk

The American Lutheran Church, for its "Vision for Mission" program, 1986-87, requested a theme hymn for the church-wide, year-long evangelism effort, coupling the spiritual and social concerns of the church. The hymn emphasizes the proving of the church's confession of faith by agape and acts of charity, concern for the whole person with Christ the motivator. The refrain suggests captivating the unconverted by a display of Christ-like concern and then defining that love by the proclamation of the Gospel. The risen Christ lives in his Body, the Church.

    Carl Schalk was asked to provide a tune for this text with its unusual meter.

    The hymn can be used apart from its original purpose as a mission and witness hymn to illustrate various parallel Biblical texts.

Publications:	"Vision for Mission" program of the American Lutheran Church, 1986-87.

7 CHRIST GOES BEFORE   Irregular

Based on	John 14:6; Matthew 6:13
Theme	Christ/Discipleship
Written	18 January 1987
Suggested tune	*RIVERSIDE* by Carl Schalk

For some time I had been pondering the implications of the conclusion of the Lord's Prayer, when I wondered if there was not a parallel between the Kingdom, the Power, and the Glory and the Way, the Truth, and the Life. As I explored this possible connection, I thought of the third parallel trio: love, peace, and joy — all promised by him who is the Way, the Truth, and the Life. A request from Ascension Lutheran Church, Riverside, IL, for a text inspired by their 50th anniversary provided me with an opportunity to offer this text. The hymn is meant to begin with a refrain in the manner of "Lift high the cross." The irregular meter required a new melody, which Carl Schalk was asked to compose. The hymn was introduced on March 15, 1987, at the commissioning church.

8   COME, LORD JESUS, TO THIS PLACE   7.7.7.7.

Based on	John 2:1-11; Ephesians 5:22-32
Theme	Wedding
Written	27 June 1968
Suggested tune	*SONG 13* by Orlando Gibbons

This text was prompted by the forthcoming marriage of our first child, Susan, to Henry Raedeke, Jr. on August 11, 1968, in St. Louis. It was sung by the congregation at St. Lucas Lutheran Church to *SONG 13* by Gibbons. It was later set to a new tune by Donald Busarow and published as a vocal solo.

See notes on marriage at THIS LOVE, O CHRIST, most of which apply to this text as well.

Publications: *Come, Lord Jesus*, 1980   (See Appendix 3-A)

9   COUNT YOUR BLESSINGS, O MY SOUL   7.7.7.7.7.7.7.

Based on	Psalm 104
Theme	Praise/Thanksgiving
Written	29 April 1986
Suggested tune	*DERR, DICH LOB' DIE SEELE MEIN*

This is another of the Becker Psalter texts, a paraphrase based on Psalm 104 and presented for the first time at Grace Lutheran Church, River Forest, Illinois, on May 18, 1986. Additional notes on the series may be found at BEFORE YOUR AWESOME MAJESTY.

Publications: *Eight Psalms*, 1987   (See Appendix 2)

10   CREATOR, KEEPER, CARING LORD   8.6.8.6.8.6.

Based on   Matthew 4:23; 25:31 ff.; Luke 9:1, 2 and parallels
Theme   Wholeness/Health and Healing/Concern/Care
Written   2 August 1986
Suggested tune   *BROTHER JAMES' AIR*

To fill a need for a hymn for health and healing to be sung by congregations, institutions of care, care-takers and care-givers, this hymn was
commissioned by the Missouri District Pastors' and Teachers' Conference
of The Lutheran Church—Missouri Synod held in October 1986. It holds
up Christ as the example, motivator, and enabler of the healing ministry
of the church as it embraces the whole person and offers the gift of
wholeness and the promise of total and perfect wholeness in the life
to come.

  Because of its familiarity and associations, *BROTHER JAMES' AIR*
was selected for the introduction of the hymn. The allusions to the Good
Shepherd echoed in the tune support the image of the caring Lord to
whom this text is addressed.

11   FAR FROM THE TIME WHEN WE WERE FEW   CM (8.6.8.6.)

Based on   Deuteronomy 32:7 and parallels
Theme   Commemoration/Anniversary of The Lutheran
                  Church—Missouri Synod
Written   23 March 1972
Suggested tune   Common Meter tune

In 1972, The Lutheran Church—Missouri Synod was celebrating its 125th
anniversary. This text was requested and used in the commemoration of
that event.

12   GATHER YOUR CHILDREN, DEAR SAVIOR,
IN PEACE   10.11.11.12.

Based on   Ephesians 6:1-3
Theme   Family/Mother's Day/Father's Day
Written   23 March 1985
Suggested tune   *SLANE*

Apart from a commission from the First Congregational Church, Webster
Groves, Missouri, for a hymn for Mother's Day, I have long felt the need

for a more comprehensive hymn for Christian families that would be useful not only for Mother's Day but for other occasions as well. The importance of the family is being acknowledged more in the church and in society as it is fractured and weakened to the loss of future generations. Here was an opportunity to draw a parallel between the family of God and Christian families. *SLANE* was chosen for its familiarity and appropriateness and for its tenderness. In using this tune, the meter of this version should be noted, as other versions shorten one or more lines.

Publications: *Gather Your Children, Dear Savior, in Peace*, 1987
                 (See Appendix 3-A)

13   GIVE GLORY, ALL CREATION   7.8.7.8.7.6.7.6.7.6.7.7.7.

Based on	Psalm 103
Theme	Adoration/Praise
Written	25 August 1985
Suggested tune	*NUN LOB, MEIN SEEL, DEN HERREN*

This paraphrase of Psalm 103 was requested for the Becker Psalter series and was presented for the first time at Grace Lutheran Church, River Forest, Illinois, September 29, 1985. For additional commentary on the series, see note on BEFORE YOUR AWESOME MAJESTY.

Publications: *Eight Psalms*, 1987   (See Appendix 2)

14   GO, MY CHILDREN, WITH MY BLESSING   8.4.8.4.8.8.8.4.

Based on	Ephesians 6:1-4
Theme	Dismissal/Close of Worship/Benediction/Baptism/ Peace
Written	26 July 1983
Suggested tune	*AR HYD Y NOS*

Concordia Publishing House was looking for a text that would make the charming and popular Welsh tune, *AR HYD Y NOS*, available for daytime use, broadening its usage beyond its traditional association with an evening text. To me the soft and contemplative melody suggested a setting of the benediction as a hymn of dismissal. To set it apart from other versifications of the benediction, I placed the words of the hymn into the mouth of the blessing triune God dismissing the congregation after worship while drawing together a review of the events that transpired during the service. Quite unconsciously, this hymn became the counterpart of "Now the silence," which previews what is about to take place in the worship service. This hymn, either in its entirety or by the selection of certain stanzas, is suitable for close of worship, post-baptism and post-communion, benediction, and other occasions.

Concordia published this text as an alternative to "God who made the earth and heaven."

Publications: (See Appendix 3-A)
Go, My Children, With My Blessing, 1984
Go, My Children, With My Blessing, 1987

15 GOD OF THE SPARROW   5.4.6.7.7.

Based on	1 John 4:7-12; 1 Thessalonians 5:18; Psalm 136
Theme	Gratitude/Service/Christian Life
Written	27 October 1983
Suggested tune	*CONCORDIA* by David Christian
	ROEDER by Carl Schalk

Having been fascinated for more than 40 years in the ministry by the proper and effective motivation for Christian service, a request from Concordia Lutheran Church of Kirkwood, Missouri, provided an opportunity to compose a hymn text that would provoke answers from the users of the hymn as to why and how God's creatures (and children) are to serve him. The Law of God demands perfect love from every creature; the love of God and the Gospel coax a willing response of love as an expression of gratitude. "We love because he first loved us." God's adopted family responds both as creatures and as children, thus fulfilling the expectations of the Law with the fruits of the Spirit, and in doing so "saying" with actions something of significance to God and the world.

Concordia congregation introduced this hymn during its celebration of its 110th anniversary with a tune composed by organist and choir director David Christian. Another setting has been made by Carl Schalk, also fitting the mood of the text. Alternate readings are provided in the fourth and fifth stanzas to accommodate the musical accents, with my personal preference for the original wording.

Publications: *Hymnal Supplement II*, 1987   (See Appendix 1)

16   GOD, WHO BUILT THIS WONDROUS PLANET   8.7.8.7.8.7.

Based on	1 Peter 2:4-10
Theme	The Church/Sanctuary/Worship/Dedication of a Church
Written	1 March 1986
Suggested tune	*REAVIS BARRACKS* by Thomas Leeseburg-Lange *ASCENDED TRIUMPH* by Henry V. Gerike

Peter compares the building of the Body of Christ, the Church, to the structure of a temple. Christ and St. Paul also use the same metaphor. For the dedication of its new church building, Holy Trinity Church, located at Union and Reavis Barracks Roads in suburban St. Louis, commissioned a hymn for the occasion to be based on the 1 Peter text. Other related allusions to the church were incorporated into the text.

To be sure that the congregation could sing the hymn without difficulty, it was written with the tune *ASCENDED TRIUMPH* by Henry V. Gerike in mind, hence the same meter and rhyme scheme as in "Up through endless ranks of angels." However, when the text was completed, the organist, Thomas Leeseberg-Lange prepared an original tune for the hymn, *REAVIS BARRACKS*. The melody was picked up enthusiastically by the celebrating congregation at its dedication service May 18, 1986.

17   HERE IS THE LIVING PROOF, GOOD LORD   C.M.

Based on	1 Samuel 7:12; Acts 20:28; 1 Peter 1:18, 19
Theme	Mortgage burning
Written	20 April 1987
Suggested tune	*ST. ANNE* *ST. PETER*

St. Lucas Lutheran Church, St. Louis, requested a text to a familiar tune on the occasion of its mortgage burning on April 26, 1987. The parallels with our indebtedness to God, and the atonement for all our debts by the blood of Christ were obvious, as well as the injunction to owe no one anything but love (Romans 13:8). The hymn was sung to ST. ANNE for its suggested reference to "O God, our help in ages past."

18   HOW COULD I HURT YOU SO?   6.6.8.4.4.4.8.

Based on   Matthew 26:75; Psalms 32 and 51
Theme   Penitence/Restoration
Written   23 June 1980
Suggested tune   *LOVE UNKNOWN*

A spontaneous composition for no special occasion. A song that expressed
my thoughts as I reviewed the enormous number of wasted opportunities
and regretted denials of my Lord's friendship over six decades. This song
was inspired by John Ireland's plaintive tune, *LOVE UNKNOWN*.

19   HOW MEAGER AND MUNDANE   6.6.8.4.4.4.8.

Based on   Luke 12:15-21; John 14:1-4; Romans 8:16-23
Theme   Eternal values/Heaven
Written   27 June 1980
Suggested tune   *LOVE UNKNOWN*

Life is never the same after a close encounter with death. As a pastor, I
witnessed mortality and how individuals dealt with it. And when I myself
suffered cardiac arrest, my own values were tested, and my life and career
fell into eternal perspective. This text was my observation of the short-
sightedness of a life that does not look to eternity. It is not an escape
from reality, but an infrequent acknowledgment that this life is temporal
and that it must be lived in the hope that transforms death from a dead
end into the launching of the eternal adventure for which we are preparing. I did not know in 1980 that I would undergo three major operations
in the next six years and a second cardiac arrest. The extension of life I
was graciously granted allowed me to write many of the hymns in this
collection. This song was also inspired by *LOVE UNKNOWN*, the John
Ireland melody, and was set to that tune's meter.

20 HOW PLEASANT, LORD,
WHEN BROTHERS LIVE   CM (8.6.8.6.)

Based on	Psalm 131:1; John 17:20-23; Ephesians 4:1-16
Theme	Church/Unity/Peace/Renewal
Written	11 January 1971
Suggested tune	*ST. PETER* or other CM

On the eve of the split in The Lutheran Church—Missouri Synod, as the
storm clouds were gathering, I was moved to write this hymn, echoing
Christ's passionate high priestly prayer in John 17, the strong exhortations
of St. Paul to the Ephesians (chapter 4) and Psalm 131:1, which my
mother used to quote when my brothers and I would quarrel, and the
Slovak hymn based on that verse, which I translated as "How lovely and
how pleasant." The word "brothers" reveals the date of composition,
when the movement against sexist terminology was just beginning to
assert itself. To my knowledge this hymn has not been sung, though its
subject matter still applies in a fractured church.

21 I PRAISE YOU, LORD, IN EVERY HOUR   8.4.7.8.4.7.4.4.4.4.7.

Based on	Psalm 30
Theme	Praise/Restoration
Written	27 February 1986
Suggested tune	*ICH PREIS DICH, HERR*

This contemporary paraphrase of Psalm 30 was prepared for the Becker
Psalter series and was first presented at Grace Lutheran Church, River
Forest, Illinois, on March 16, 1986. For additional commentary on the ser-
ies, see notes under BEFORE YOUR AWESOME MAJESTY.

Publications: *Eight Psalms*, 1987   (See Appendix 2)

22 IN HOPELESSNESS AND NEAR DESPAIR   8.7.8.7.8.8.7.

Based on	Psalm 130
Theme	Repentance/Forgiveness
Written	9 December 1985
Suggested tune	*AUS TIEFER NOT*

This contemporary paraphrase of Psalm 130 was also prepared for the
Becker Psalter series and was first presented at Grace Lutheran Church,

River Forest, Illinois, on February 16, 1986. For additional commentary, see notes on BEFORE YOUR AWESOME MAJESTY.

Publications: *Eight Psalms*, 1987   (See Appendix 2)

23   LET US PRAISE OUR GRACIOUS GOD   7.7.7.7. and Alleluias

Based on	Psalm 34:17-22
Theme	Commemoration/Church in the New World
Written	7 October 1983
Suggested tune	*SONNE DER GERECHTIGKEIT*

Beginning in the 80s of the last century, one-third of the population of Slovakia (the eastern third of present-day Czechoslovakia) emigrated from their homeland, mainly to America, to escape more than nine centuries of political oppression and economic distress. Whether Roman Catholic or Lutheran, they brought with them a strong set of Christian values and a devout faith and established congregations soon after their arrival. For the commemoration of the first Slovak Lutheran congregation's 100th anniversary in the New World, Holy Trinity Lutheran Church of Streator, Illinois, requested a commemorative hymn. The choice of the hymn tune was guided by the fact that Holy Trinity congregation traces its roots to the Slavic Reformation, whose Bohemian Brethren branch produced many hymns and melodies, one of the most festive of which is *SONNE DER GERECHTIGKEIT.*

Some of the references in this hymn coincide with those explained in the notes on the translation of the Slovak hymn, CHRISTIANS, LET US REMEMBER.

24   LORD, AS YOU TAUGHT US ONCE TO PRAY   10 lines of 8'

Based on	Luke 11:1-4; John 15:12-17
Theme	Love Divine/Unity in Christ
Written	30 January 1978
Suggested tune	*ANNIE LYTLE* by Lloyd Pfautsch

This was one of three hymns commissioned by the Hymn Society of America in 1978 in memory of Annie Lytle Miller (1918-1977) and set to a tune by Lloyd Pfautsch. The theme was one of my favorites and one, I feel, has to be constantly re-emphasized in the Christian community: love for one's neighbor inspired by God's love for us and our love for God.

If we love the God whom we do not see, how should we not love our neighbor whom we can see?

The repeated refrain in each stanza bears traces of the villanelle, which I would some day like to see used in its full form in a sacred song. I would hope to be forgiven the use of the generic word for humankind in stanza three for the sake of succinctness and rhyme in the third stanza. I have not yet found an adequate poetic substitute for "man" that does not sound artificial while drawing undue attention to itself and diverting attention from the rest of the poem.

Publications: *Three Hymns for 1979*, 1979   (See Appendix 1)

25   LORD, I MUST PRAISE YOU   Irregular

Based on	Psalm 111
Theme	Praise/Gratitude/Trust
Written	4 December 1985
Suggested tune	*ICH WILL VON HERZEN DANKEN GOTT*

This contemporary paraphrase of Psalm 111 was one of eight requested for the Becker/Schuetz cantata series and was presented for the first time at Grace Lutheran Church, River Forest, Illinois, on January 12, 1986. Background notes on the series may be found at BEFORE YOUR AWE-SOME MAJESTY.

Publications: *Eight Psalms*, 1987   (See Appendix 2)

26   NOW, AT THE PEAK OF WONDER   7.7.7.7.5.5.6.

Based on	1 Peter 2:9, 10
Theme	The Christian Community/Anniversary
Written	20 August 1981
Suggested tune	*SAPPINGTON* by Richard W. Gieseke

To mark the 25th anniversary of its organization, the Lutheran Church of the Resurrection in Sappington, Missouri, commissioned this hymn to depict the purpose and activities of a Christian congregation. The hymn's use is not restricted to the anniversary of a church, though it can be used as such for anniversaries other than the 25th, or to celebrate the community of Christ in mission.

Richard W. Gieseke, while organist and choir director at Resurrection Church, prepared a concertato arrangement of the hymn for congregation, choir, timpani, organ, and brass, and named it *SAPPINGTON* after the church's location.

Publications: *Now at the Peak of Wonder*, 1983
                 (See Appendix 3-A)

27   NOW THE SILENCE   Irregular

Based on   Habakkuk 2:20; Psalm 122:1
Theme   Entrance/Worship/Communion
Written   12 March 1968
Suggested tune   *NOW* by Carl Schalk

If there was one hymn text that proved a catalyst for my hymn writing, it was "Now the silence," already alluded to in the introduction to this anthology. And Carl Schalk must be given the credit for recognizing the potential of this unusual text as a hymn. Its subsequent acceptance convinced me (and evidently many others) that hymns could take on new forms and yet perform their function in congregational worship. In the nearly two decades since the text came to me while shaving, I have been discovering roots and hints in past experiences and Scriptural passages and stories. The opening line of one of Hviezdoslav's lyrics (mentioned in the introduction), "Wish me silence, wish me peace," surfaced 25 years later as "Now the silence, now the peace." And the reverse order of the Doxology/Benediction not only expressed the order in which I pictured the Trinity coming to us in worship, but also the order in which the Incarnation took place: the vistation of the Virgin Mary by the Holy Spirit, then the Son's epiphany as the incarnate Word, followed by the universal blessing that is bestowed upon all in whom this same process occurs.

Carl Schalk's collaboration with me on this hymn and others prompts an expression of appreciation to him and to all musicians, without whom hymn texts, no matter how good, would die. And Schalk's setting *NOW* was the beginning of a congenial collaboration which continues to amaze me.

Publications: *Worship Supplement*, 1979
                 Contemporary Worship: Hymns (1), 1969
                 Johannine Hymnal, 1970
                 Contemporary Worship: (4), Hymns for Baptism and
                     Communion, 1972
                 The Hymnal of the United Church of Christ, 1974

Publications:	*Worship II*, 1975
(Continued)	*Ecumenical Praise*, 1977
	Lutheran Book of Worship, 1978
	Hymns in Large Print, 1979
	Choirbook for Saints and Sinners, 1980
	Catholic Book of Worship II, 1980
	Welshire Hymns, 1980
	Hymnal Supplement, 1984
	The Hymnal 1982, 1985
	Worship: A Hymnal and Service Book for Roman Catholics, 1986
	Now, 1986 (See Appendix 3-A)
	Hymnal Supplement II, 1987
	Songs for a Gospel People, 1987
	Now the Silence, 1987 (See Appendix 3-A)
	New Songs of Praise 3, 1987

(See Appendix 1 for complete data on hymnals, ref. by date)

28   O DAY OF DAYS, THE DAY I FOUND   LM (8.8.8.8.)

Based on	John 1:35-51; Galatians 1:11-2:21
Theme	Discipleship/Commitment/Confirmation/Rededication
Written	5 October 1972
Suggested tune	*WINCHESTER NEW*

Now and again the remembrance of God's grace in Christ stuns me into an awareness and appreciation of the relationship I enjoy with God. This hymn is meant to jog my memory and that of other children of God and prompt thanksgiving and rededication. It can also serve as a hymn for confirmation and commitment to service.

29   O GOD, ETERNAL FATHER, LORD   8.8.8. and Alleluia

Based on	Revelation 4:11; John 14:26; 1 Peter 1:2
Theme	Holy Trinity/Credo/Doxology
Written	20 June 1969
Suggested tune	*GELOBT SEI GOTT*

Inspired by numerous versified Credos that occupy so many liturgical hymnals, this abbreviated three-stanza "credo" can serve as a brief confessional or doxological minute in one's daily devotions. Line 2 in stanza two still uses the generic word for humanity, betraying the date of its composition.

30   PASS IN REVIEW   10.10.10.10.

Based on	Isaiah 62:6; 2 Corinthians 5:20; Hebrews 13:17
Theme	Ministry/Anniversary
Written	2 April 1986
Suggested tune	*OLD 124TH*

For more than a generation, pastors' ordinations and installations in our church have used one of the few available hymns pertaining to the office of the holy ministry, "God of the prophets, bless the prophets' sons," to *OLD 124TH*. Even fewer hymns were available for ministers celebrating anniversaries or retirements. So I welcomed the request to write a hymn for the golden (50th) anniversary of Dr. John Kovac at St. Lucas Lutheran Church, St. Louis, on May 25, 1986. Various aspects of the holy ministry are reviewed as the life and career of God's servant are commemorated. The text was set to *OLD 124TH*, which in turn was to call up associations with the Denis Wortman text, "God of the prophets."

31   PEACE CAME TO EARTH   10.10.10.8.8.

Based on	Luke 2:14; Galatians 4:4; Ephesians 2:14
Theme	Incarnation/Christmas
Written	24 January 1984
Suggested tune	*SCHNEIDER* by Paul Manz

As Pastor Theodore F. Schneider's congregation, The Lutheran Church of the Good Shepherd in Lancaster, Pennsylvania, was preparing to celebrate the 25th anniversary of its spiritual shepherd's ordination, Dr. Karl E. Moyer, organist and choir director, requested a hymn based on a memorable sermon Pastor Schneider had preached on an earlier Christmas Eve on Galatians 4:4. The hymn was to laud the Incarnation rather than the charms of Christmas, and was to be presented as a gift to the church and to Pastor Schneider at the anniversary service on Trinity Sunday, June 17, 1984. I was able to attend the commemorative service, one of the few times I was privileged to witness the introduction of a new hymn.

   Since Pastor Schneider's favorite theme also happened to be mine, I was pleased to write a text that would explore more of the implications of the Incarnation than are ordinarily found in Christmas texts, for example, the communion that takes place in the Sacrament of the Altar, and the incorporation of believers into the Body of Christ. One is dealing with the very essence of Christianity, in which the Incarnation is absolutely essential to the world's redemption and the union of the creature with the Creator and Redeemer. The repetition of Immanuel is meant to impress its literal meaning on the singer of the hymn with its numerous implications.

Since the meter of the text does not fit any existing melody, Paul Manz was commissioned to write a new one, a very fitting one as it turned out, and named it *SCHNEIDER* for evident reasons.

32   SEE THIS WONDER IN THE MAKING   LM (8.8.8.8.)
Trochaic

Based on	Romans 6:3-6; Colossians 2:12; James 1:18; 1 Peter 3:2; Titus 3:4-7
Theme	Infant Baptism/Regeneration
Written	5 August 1984
Suggested tune	*TRYGGARE KAN INGEN VARA*

Hymnody can help restore Baptism to its central place in the life and worship of God's people. As such, it can open the mind and heart to a range of considerations of this sacramental means of grace often forgotten, overlooked, or ignored by too many Christians, whereas it can and should be the source of daily comfort and an incentive to daily repentance and the renewal of one's membership in the Body of Christ and participation in the crucifixion/redemption of Christ, as attested to by such important passages as those listed above, the contemplation of which can open floodgates of inspiration for other hymns on the subject of baptism.

The validity of Baptism as a sacrament has served God's children, infant, young, and old, since apostolic times, and has proved to be a refuge and an earnest of their divine regeneration and adoption.

Lines 1 and 2 of the fourth stanza translate the thought of an old European folk saying associated with infant baptism: "We took you to church a heathen; we brought you home a Christian."

This particular hymn text was prompted by a long-standing need for more contemporary baptismal hymns, and as a substitute for "Children of the heavenly Father," set to the charming Swedish folk tune usually only indirectly related to the rite of baptism. This new text, specifically connected with baptism and tied to the Swedish tune, affords an opportunity to define how that familial relationship comes about.

33 THEN THE GLORY   Irregular

Based on	1 Corinthians 2:9; 2 Corinthians 4:13-18
Theme	Resurrection/Eternal Life
Written	17 February 1970, revised 10 January 1986
Suggested tune	*NOW*, by Carl Schalk

Subsequent to the writing of "Now the silence" I wrote this "sequel" to
the hymn that summarizes the elements of a worship service. If all that
(in "Now the silence") is happening in our worship of the Lord here,
what awaits us in our worship when we reach the end of our redemption
in the glory of the world to come? One can only begin to imagine in a
hymn of this kind some of the wonders C. S. Lewis explores in *The
Weight of Glory*.

 This hymn must of course be sung to *NOW* by Carl Schalk.

34 THIS CHILD OF OURS   8.8.8.8. Refrain

Based on	John 3:5; Matthew 18:10; 19:14
Theme	Baptism
Written	5 August 1984
Suggested tune	*THIS CHILD OF OURS* by Richard W. Gieseke

A baptismal hymn for their child Sarah was requested by Richard and
Susan Gieseke while Richard was organist and choirmaster at Resurrection
Lutheran Church in Sappington, Missouri, a suburb of St. Louis. I wanted
to point out the dual parentage of our children as the result of Baptism.
Though our child becomes God's child by means of the washing of
regeneration, it still remains our child, but with much more significance
than it would have as just a human offspring, though that is miracle
enough. Combine that wonder with the miracle of spiritual rebirth, and
the worth of the child increases fantastically.

35 THIS IS A TIME FOR BANNERS AND BELLS   9.7.9.7. Refrain

Based on	Revelation 21:5; 2 Corinthians 5:17
Theme	Commemoration/Church Anniversary
Written	20 February 1983
Suggested tune	*GLORIA DEI* by Paul Manz

Gloria Dei Lutheran Church of St. Paul, Minnesota, built its 75th anniversary celebration in 1983 around the theme: "Behold, I make all things

new" (Rev. 21:5), a refrain of Paul's statement in 2 Cor. 5:17. The church is Christ's Bride, his new creation, and the community of believers is witness to that regenerating power of God and the transforming power of Christ. This hymn can serve any congregation marking an anniversary by omitting the fifth stanza, which compares the diamond (75th) anniversary to a diamond in Christ's crown.

Paul Manz was commissioned to write a tune for the hymn which he named *GLORIA DEI.*

36 THIS LOVE, O CHRIST   10.8.10.8.10.10.

Based on	Ephesians 5:21-33; Revelation 19:7-9
Theme	Wedding/Marriage
Written	1 July 1977
Suggested tune	*THIS LOVE* by Donald Busarow

In an age when secular models for marriage are selfish and romantically unrealistic, when the meaning of marital love is diluted and distorted (as it is in most popular songs), I welcomed the opportunity to hold up for the Christian couple exchanging vows the model set by the Scriptures: the totally committed union between Christ and his Bride, the Church, as depicted in Isaiah, the Song of Solomon, Hosea, Ephesians 5 and Revelation 19. Surely the power to achieve an approximation of that ideal union is available from the one who designed marriage and blesses the couple who commit themselves to its ideal and purpose. The practice of daily confession in the home is the mark of the Spirit's presence and activity. In displaying and nurturing this model for marriage, the church is as much a savior in respect to this fundamental element as it is in its concern for peace and justice, for the poor, the homeless, and the hungry. In a Christian marriage these virtues and values are nourished for the happiness of families and the health of society.

This wedding song was requested by Concordia Publishing House for a collection of wedding hymns, and Donald Busarow was asked to set the text to music.

One small revision should be noted in 2:4. The line originally read: "Admiring, trusting, faithful unto death," which had two extra syllables.

Publications: *This Love*, 1980   (See Appendix 3-A)

- 163 -

37   THIS TOUCH OF LOVE   4.4.8.4.4.4.

Based on   Matthew 26:26-29; Luke 22:14-20
Theme   Post-Communion
Written   3 March 1971
Suggested tune   *COMMUNION* by Carl Schalk

Not always, not even often, much less often enough am I aware of what
is happening in that high and tender meeting between my Lord and
myself in the Sacrament of Holy Communion. I would hope that a hymn
of this kind would heighten the consciousness of those who have just
communed of the special nature of the occasion. Carl Schalk composed a
melody for this text in April 1987.

Publications: *This Touch of Love*, 1988   (See Appendix 3-A)

38   THOUGH MOUNTAINS QUAKE AND
OCEANS ROAR   8.7.8.7.6.6.6.6.7.

Based on   Psalm 46
Theme   Trust
Written   29 September 1985
Suggested tune   *EIN FESTE BURG*

At the risk of presumption, this contemporary paraphrase of Psalm 46
was requested for the Becker Psalter series of cantatas presented at Grace
Lutheran Church, River Forest, Illinois, on October 27, 1985. I trust it
may claim a place, though inferior, next to the Reformer's with gratitude
for the use of his mighty melody. Additional notes on the cantata series
may be found under BEFORE YOUR AWESOME MAJESTY.

Publications: *Eight Psalms*, 1987   (See Appendix 2)

39   UP THROUGH ENDLESS RANKS OF ANGELS   8.7.8.7.8.7.

Based on   Luke 24:50-53; Acts 1:9-11
Theme   Ascension (Hymn of the Day)
Written   25 May 1973
Suggested tune   *ASCENDED TRIUMPH* by Henry V. Gerike

During the preparation of the *Lutheran Book of Worship* (1978), Augsburg Publishing House asked for an Ascension hymn to go with *OUR*

LADY TRONDHEIM, hence the metric structure of the text. Into that format I gathered a number of implications of the Ascension as they apply to the followers of Christ, who recall his departure and await his promised return. Taking the Scriptural phenomenological viewpoint, I originally began the text with the word "Up." The publishers, however, preferred to avoid the three-tiered universe imagery and so substituted the word "There," in which version they published a setting by Carl Schalk. When the Inter-Lutheran Commission on Worship chose the text as the hymn of the day for Ascension, the original opening preposition was restored and a last-minute substitution for both *OUR LADY TRONDHEIM* and the Carl Schalk tune was made: *ASCENDED TRIUMPH* by Henry V. Gerike, the festive tune almost always used with the text since that time.

Publications: *There Through Endless Ranks of Angels*, 1974
                    (See Appendix 3-A)
                 Up Through Endless Ranks of Angels, 1976
                    (See Appendix 3-A)
                 Lutheran Book of Worship, 1978
                    [159: Hymn of the day]   (See Appendix 1)
                 Lutheran Worship, 1982 [152: Hymn of the day]
                    (See Appendix 1)
                 Up Through Endless Ranks of Angels, 1986
                    (See Appendix 3-A)
                 Hymnal Supplement II, 1987   (See Appendix 1)

40   WHERE SHEPHERDS LATELY KNELT   12.12.10.10.

Based on   Luke 2:8-18
Theme   Christmas
Written   9 July 1986
Suggested tune   *MANAGER SONG* by Carl Schalk

Another request from Augsburg Publishing House for a Christmas song for their Christmas Annual, this time for the 1987 edition, like that which resulted in "Before the marvel of this night" in the 1981 annual, prompted the composition of this hymn on the adoration of the Christ Child in the manger. Once again I wondered what fresh approach and contemporary application could be made of that central event in history. Rather than report the event again in the third person, as so many Christmas songs do, I placed myself in spirit at that poor manger bed and reviewed the implications of that visit in my life and future and in that of my fellow human beings. I have struggled, and more so as I grow older, with the incomprehensibility of that event and of my connection with it, and with each commemoration of that miracle becoming more routine, though its impact on God's heart remains the means of my salvation. I pictured myself at the opposite side of the event from Isaiah and his prophecy (9:6, 7), applying the same promise to myself as a late-arriving pilgrim.

The original metrical structure of the hymn was 6.6.6.6.4.4.2, which Carl Schalk reformed to make a three-line hymn, 12.12.10. with a repetition of the last line. Once again Schalk captured the mood and style of the text, while making the lines more fluent and giving additional attention to the crucial refrain.

Publications: "Where shepherds lately knelt" in *Christmas*, 1987
                  (See Appendix 2)
            Where Shepherds Lately Knelt, 1987
                  (See Appendix 3-A)

41   WHERE YOU ARE, THERE IS LIFE   6.6.6.8.8.6.4.

Based on	John 1:4; 14:6, 23, 27
Theme	New Creation/Union with God
Written	5 December 1982
Suggested tune	(None extant)

This is an uncommissioned, unassigned hymn text, for which as yet no tune has been composed. It recalls the union of the believer with God, the first three stanzas referring to the persons of the Trinity, and the last a doxology. I debated about the use of the word "umbilical" in the first stanza, trusting it would not seem to have been chosen for effect rather than meaning. To me it expresses the generating place of the Word in our rebirth as God's children. Lacking rhymes, it is my hope that the rhythm, the refrain, and the melody will take care of that omission.

42   WHO COULD HAVE DREAMT A LAND LIKE THIS?   Irregular

Based on	Proverbs 11:11; 14:34; Deuteronomy 8:10-18; 1 Timothy 2:1-4
Theme	Nation
Written	15 March 1975
Suggested tune	*WIE SCHÖN LEUCHTET*

Clifton Lutheran Church of Marblehead, Massachusetts, wished to commission a national hymn commemorating the Bicentennial of the

Declaration of Independence in 1976, and to dedicate it to the town of Marblehead, where the first German Lutherans landed in 1630, a century and a half before the Constitution was signed. Dr. Cyril Wismar conveyed the request for a hymn to be dedicated to Marblehead in memory of Peter Stengel.

I wrote the text to the classic Lutheran chorale *Wie schön leuchtet* for three reasons: 1) It is a strong, stately, and familiar melody; 2) the hymn was commissioned by a Lutheran church to remember the Lutheran immigrants to Marblehead in 1630, for whom this Queen of Chorales recalls the spirit and words of that hymn, and 3) to make this an ethnic tribute to a land of opportunity, where German came close to becoming the official language of the country.

The gifts of freedom, peace, and prosperity are from the hands of a gracious God, priceless gifts to be recognized and received with thanksgiving and responsibility. A national hymn must be honestly patriotic without being jingoistic or blindly chauvinistic. In light of our blessings and privileges, we have much to be humble about. The second stanza strikes the necessary penitential note. That properly recognized, we can go on to celebrate our anniversaries with joy and new dedication to our ideals.

Paul Manz wrote a counter-melody for the chorale tune that can be sung by itself or together with the familiar chorale. Whether intentional or not, the Manz melody begins with the same key notes as *The Starspangled Banner*. The hymn was sung in Marblehead during the bicentennial year as well as throughout the country in Lutheran churches using a special bicentennial order of worship.

43   WHO IS THIS WHO COMES FROM NOWHERE?

Based on	Hebrews 7; Luke 24:25-27; Matthew 5:2-12; 25:34
Theme	Discipleship
Written	10 February 1987
Suggested tune	(None extant)

When Paul Westermeyer, on behalf of Ascension Lutheran Church, Riverside, Illinois, requested a hymn to mark the congregation's 75th anniversary in 1987, this was one of two texts that I wrote. The other was "Christ goes before." The hymn was not to deal specifically with the anniversary, but was meant to hold up to the congregation the mission of the church as it is directed by the ascended Lord. In this text I imagined Christ coming into history and into people's lives as if from nowhere. I thought of the comparison with Melchizedek, the subject of Hebrews 7, the statement of Christ's contemporaries: "Is this not the carpenter's son?" and "What good can come out of Nazareth?" But this is the promised

Messiah awaited by Israel and sought unknowingly by pagans. The second stanza summarizes the risen Christ's exposition of the Old Testament prophecies to the dismayed disciples on the road to Emmaus. The third connects the petitions of the Lord's Prayer with the Great Commission, and the fourth ties the Beatitudes to the final commendation of those who follow Christ, who became their Savior in order that their joy might be full.

The lengthening of the third last line of the stanzas was intended to keep the last four lines moving toward the climactic last line.

44   YOU ARE THE KING   14 lines of 10'

Based on   Isaiah 6:1-6
Theme   Ministry/Service
Written   20 November 1979
Suggested tune   *FAIRMOUNT* by Donald Busarow

This text responds to the request of the session and congregation of Fairmount Presbyterian Church of Cleveland Heights, Ohio, for a hymn honoring their dedicated minister of music, Dr. H. Wells Near, to be based on Isaiah 6:1-8. Aware of two great hymns on this text, Luther's majestic one-stanza narrative hymn, "Isaiah, Mighty Seer" and Reginald Heber's universally familiar hymn to the Trinity, "Holy, Holy, Holy," I decided to take a different approach by dealing with God's call to service in the Kingdom. Having wanted for years to write a hymn in sonnet form, this theme seemed to fit that unusual form admirably: the Shakespearean sonnet of three quatrains and a closing couplet. Since the melody was to be composed after the text, this poetic form was chosen. The hymn is to be understood at different levels, just as the calling of Isaiah came in a vision that lifted him above the act of commissioning to glimpse the very holiness of the triune God and his consuming love for his creatures. One example of a dual meaning is the phrase, "crossed the gaping gulf" referring to the cross as the bridge God provides as the bridge to us and to himself.

Donald Busarow accepted the challenge of writing a tune for this unusual hymn form, which he named *FAIRMOUNT* after the commissioning church's location. The hymn was presented to Dr. Near on May 18, 1980.

45 YOU ARE THE ROCK

8.7.8.7.8.8.7.

Based on   Ephesians 2:19-22
Theme   Church Anniversary/Commemoration
Written   5 February 1979
Suggested tune   *ES IST DAS HEIL*

This hymn for the anniversary of a congregation was written to com-
memorate the centennial of Zion Lutheran Church, Dallas, Texas, in 1979.
ES IST DAS HEIL was chosen as the melody for its familiarity and associations as a description of the nature and glory of the Gospel, which this
church was called to plant and proclaim in the pioneering years of the
state of Texas. The text ties that local congregation to the Una Sancta in
its purpose and mission, in its recruitment of members for the Body
of Christ.

46 YOU ARE THE SHEPHERD

CM (8.6.8.6.)

Based on   Psalm 23; John 10:11; 20:16, 17; Acts 20:28
Theme   Social service/Care of the elderly
Written   5 September 1985
Suggested tune   *ST. ANNE*
                 ST. PETER

The forgotten and neglected elderly people of God are remembered in this
text commemorating the 80th anniversary of the Lutheran Altenheim
Society of Missouri in 1985. Our care of the elderly should be inspired by
the Shepherd who cares for all his sheep, including those who once were
with young and who must now be carried by other "shepherds" as they
were when they were lambs. *ST. ANNE* was the first choice of tune,
because of its familiarity and connotations among the residents of this
retirement and nursing facility. The Lutheran Altenheim Society has been
a model of Christian charity for eight decades.

47 YOU, JESUS, ARE MY SHEPHERD TRUE   8.7.8.7.8.8.7.

Based on   Psalm 23
Theme   Trust/Guidance/Protection
Written   10 March 1986
Suggested tune   *DER HERR IST MEIN GETREUER HIRT*

This contemporary paraphrase of Psalm 23 was one of eight in the
Becker Psalter series presented at Grace Lutheran Church, River Forest,
Illinois, on April 20, 1986. For additional notes on the series, see BEFORE
YOUR AWESOME MAJESTY.

Publications: *Eight Psalms*, 1987   (See Appendix 2)

48 READINGS FROM ACTS, VERSIFIED   CM (8.6.8.6.)

Based on   Easter cycle lectionary readings from the Book of Acts
Theme   Easter life
Written   15 September 1980
Suggested tune   Easter Motet Series, by Christopher Tye
                  (see note below)

Christopher Tye (c. 1505-1572), musical tutor to King Edward VI and
organist of the Chapel Royal under Queen Elizabeth, rendered the first
fourteen chapters of the Book of Acts into meter, which he then set to
music. Augsburg Publishing House requested new texts for three sets of
six Tye motets each for use on the Sundays of Easter and based on the
First Lesson as appointed in the three-year lectionary (all from the Book
of Acts) in the *Lutheran Book of Worship* and *Lutheran Worship*. The
texts were prepared for a three-set collection published by Augsburg in
three successive years under the title *Easter Motets:* Series B in 1984,
Series C in 1985, and Series A in 1986.

Publications: *Readings from Acts, Versified*   (See Appendix 3-A)

49 GIFT OF JOY   Irregular

Based on   Luke 1:78, 79
Theme   Advent/Christmas
Written   15 July 1977
Suggested tune   Anthem by Albert Rykken Johnson

This Advent/Christmas text was composed to fit an anthem by Albert
Rykken Johnson, of Brainerd, Minnesota, set to a text originally entitled,
"In a far lonely manger," which determined the special meter of this
alternate text.

50 I HAVE A FATHER YOU WOULD LIKE   CM (8.6.8.6.)

Based on   Matthew 11:25, 26; 21:15; 2 Kings 5:1-4
Theme   Children/Witness/Evangelism
Written   15 September 1981
Suggested tune   Extant or new CM tune

I must have remembered George Shibata, a Japanese-American (Nisei)
seminary classmate of mine, who, I learned, had become a Christian as a
nine-year-old boy in California, when a Christian playmate invited him to
Sunday school. After graduating from the seminary in 1945, Shibata
spent most of his ministry serving the Japanese people, and at this time
is stationed in Okinawa. And there are the biblical examples of Naaman's
maid recommending the God of Israel to her master, and the little children
singing hosannas to Christ on Palm Sunday. These instances of child
"evangelism" were in the back of my mind as I wrote this simple song in
response to a stated need for a children's personal evangelism program
the church was planning, though it has remained unused to date. It can
be sung to any suitable common meter melody until a new one is written
for it.

51 O DEAREST FRIEND   12.10.12.10.12.10.12.12.

Based on   John 21:15-17; Psalm 51
Theme   Repentance/Restoration/Commitment
Written   24 January 1976
Suggested tune   *LONDONDERRY AIR*

When I was five, and we lived in Racine, Wisconsin, my father took me
to Milwaukee to hear a concert by Fritz Kreisler, renowned as one of the

world's greatest violinists. As I shook the hand of the virtuoso backstage, I was determined to play the violin, too. In a few weeks I was taking lessons on my three-quarter-size violin. Seven years later my teacher assigned me Kreisler's poignant transcription of Londonderry Air, which has haunted me ever since. Fifty years after the Kreisler concert I was moved by that bittersweet Irish air to write a text depicting that deeper relationship between the Christian and his/her dearest Friend and the vulnerability of that friendship as it experiences closeness and disappointment, with always the hope of restoration. This was illustrated for me at least in the Garden test of Peter, the chosen friend who let down his dearest Friend and yet could hope to be given another chance. The first stanza can stand by itself, or, combined with the second, can echo the similar experience of David as expressed in Psalm 51. It was the weekly singing of the Offertory based on Psalm 51:10-12 that became my frequent penitential prayer.

52   ROCK-A-BYE, MY DEAR LITTLE BOY   12.10.8.8.8.10.

Based on	Luke 1:46-55, 2:51
Theme	Christmas/Mary's Lullaby
Written	6 July 1987
Suggested tune	Czech Carol "Hajej, nynjej" (*ROCKING*)

The charming Czech Christmas carol traditionally known as *ROCKING* translated into English a half century ago has captivated me for many years. I was, however, disappointed in the lightness of its content, pretending as it does to be sung by the maiden who composed the Magnificat. Wondering what kind of lullaby the mother of the Savior might have sung to "that holy Thing" she had borne, I wrote a new text moving the content of the carol closer to a hymn while trying to keep the simplicity and intimacy of the traditional carol.

Furthermore, since Mary was the kind of mother who "kept all these things in her heart," it is likely that she mulled over the message of Gabriel, the greeting of Elizabeth, and the prophecy of Simeon as she rocked the Infant to sleep, and wondered, as most mothers do, what would become of this special child, and what the "sword" was that would one day pierce her heart.

Still another variation occurs in the composition of this new text to an old tune: each note in the carol is given a syllable instead of the numerous slurs that appear in *ROCKING*.

53   SOMEONE SPECIAL   7.7.7.7.7.7.

Based on	Romans 8:14-17; 1 Peter 2:9, 10
Theme	Children/Self-esteem
Written	30 October 1978
Suggested tune	*SOMEONE SPECIAL* by Carl Schalk

In preparation for the Year of the Child in 1979, the Board of Parish
Education of The Lutheran Church-Missouri Synod commissioned this
hymn for children, to relate the Christian child to the various seasons of
the church year, and thereby to the life of Christ. It was introduced at the
1979 general convention of the LCMS in St. Louis, where a children's
choir sang certain stanzas in German, Spanish, and Chinese. It has been
used in various curricular materials and at parochial school teachers' con-
ferences. Three additional stanzas were composed for the Southern California Lutheran Teacher's Conference in 1986.

   Carl Schalk composed a very suitable melody for the text. The hymn
was dedicated to our three grandchildren, Daniel, Joel, and Jonathan
Raedeke, whose parents are Christian day school teachers.

| Publications: | Various Board for Parish Services publications of The Lutheran Church—Missouri Synod and of the American Lutheran Church |
| | *Someone Special*, 1987   (See Appendix 3-A) |

54   THE FRIEND I NEED   4.5.7.4.5.7.

Based on	John 15:12-17
Theme	Friendship, Divine and Human/Youth
Written	19 March 1983
Suggested tune	*AMIGO* by David Christian

Illustrating the theme of Friendship ("Amigos de Christos" for the 1983
Youth Convention of The Lutheran Church—Missouri Synod in San
Antonio, Texas, this hymn takes its inspiration from the statements of
Christ in John 15:12-17, where Christ introduces himself as the ideal
friend and the model for true friendship, inspired and motivated by Jesus,
who is addressed in the hymn.

55   ASCENDING, CHRIST RETURNS TO GOD   8.4.8.4.

Based on	John 20:17; Acts 1:4-12
Theme	Ascension
Written	18 February 1976
Translation of	*Vstoupil jest Kristus na nebe*, Old Czech, 16th cent.
Suggested tune	*ZPIVEJMEŽ VŠICKNI VESELE*

The Old Czech Ascension hymn from which this translation was made
was itself a translation of a Latin original, whose unknown origin
obviously antedates the 1636 edition of the *Cithara Sanctorum*, in which
the Slovak text appears. In its original form the hymn had 13 stanzas,
which I reduced to nine. It was evidently sung to the same melody as
Zpivejmež všickni vesele, the George Tranovsky hymn which I translated
as "Make songs of joy." (See note at that title)

56   CHRISTIANS, LET US REMEMBER   7.6.7.6.D.

Based on	Isaiah 51:1; Acts 16:9 ff.; Philippians 1:3-5; 4:15
Theme	Commemoration (Christianization of Slavs)
Written	4 March 1984
Translation of	*Pamatujmež křestane*, by Ján Kollár, 1842
Suggested tune	*VALET WILL ICH DIR GEBEN* or *HERZLICH TUT MICH VERLANGEN*

In contrast to most national heroes, the national idols of the peace-loving
Slovak people are two Macedonian missionaries who brought the Gospel
to that central European nation in the year 863. In 1983, the Slavic inhab-
itants of present-day Czechoslovakia commemorated the arrival of Cyril
(Constantine) and Methodius at the invitation of the Slovak prince Ras-
tislav, who had erected the first Christian church on Slovak soil in the
year 833. The Greek brother missionaries were welcomed and the Gospel
embraced, unlike other nations who were converted by force. Despite
their struggles with the Western popes, the brothers eventually were
granted permission to preach and conduct the liturgy in the vernacular,
for which they had created an alphabet and translated the Scriptures.
Small wonder they have been revered as the patron saints of Slovak (and
Slavic) Christians for eleven centuries. The author of this commemorative hymn celebrates the millennial anniversary of his nation's conversion
and the manner in which it was done. One is reminded of a similar conversion of the Macedonians some eight centuries prior to Cyril and
Methodius, when the request came to St. Paul in a vision, "Come over

to Macedonia and help us" (Acts 16:9 ff.). His response to that invitation marked the beginning of Paul's ministry to his beloved Philippians. By the route of the Macedonian apostles to the Slavs, I trace my own spiritual roots to St. Paul, and consequently was pleased to find this hymn text and to translate it for the millions of English-speaking descendants of that Christian nation, one-third of whose population emigrated to the United States a century ago, bringing their heritage with them.

The Slovak text was written for the 1842 Slovak Lutheran hymnal, the *Zpevník*, by Ján Kollár (1793-1852), Lutheran theologian, historian, classical poet, and national leader.

57   COME IN HOLY AWE AND TRUTH   7.8.7.8.7.7.

Based on	1 Corinthians 10:16, 17
Theme	Pre-Communion/Distribution
Written	6 October 1971, rev. 1975
Translation of	*Blízte se s náboznosti*, by Ján Bohumil Ertel
Suggested tune	*JESUS, MEINE ZUVERSICHT* or other 7.8.7.8.7.7.

This hymn comes into the English in a roundabout way. It was originally written in German by Johann Friedrich Starke (1680-1756), a German pietist pastor in Frankfurt, whom Julian describes as "a faithful follower of Spener and author of a very popular book of daily devotions (who) wrote 939 pious hymns of no poetic value" (*Dictionary of Hymnology*, New Dover Edition, 1957, p. 417). The hymn was translated into Slovak in 1745 by Jan Bohumil Ertel, a bilingual pastor in Slovakia and appeared in the 1842 *Zpevník* (Songbook) as a Communion hymn. Unable to locate the original German text, I assumed this was one of the better hymns of the 939 in Starke's collection, and that it could be further improved poetically by another translation. My interest in the hymn was drawn by its theme of Christian unity and joy and the application of the Sacrament to the life of God's people beyond the sanctuary.

58   DEAR FATHER GOD, WE RISE TO SAY   LM (8.8.8.8.)

Based on	Psalm 5:3
Theme	Morning prayer
Written	30 July 1969
Translation of	*Bože Otče, buď pochválen*, by Juraj Zábojnik, 17th cent.
Suggested tune	*PANE BOŽE, BUDIŽ CHVÁLA*, Old Czech

This Trinitarian morning hymn comes to us from the Slovak Lutheran
hymn writer, Juraj Zábojnik (1608-1672) via later editions of the *Cithara
Sanctorum*. The Old Czech melody entered the Slovak Lutheran hymnal
via the *Cantus Catholici* of 1655. Another tune from a 1576 Bohemian
Brethren hymnal is sometimes used with this hymn. Ulrich S. Leupold,
editor of *Laudamus*, requested this translation for the 1970 (4th) edition
of that Lutheran World Federation tri-lingual songbook. It was reprinted
in the 1984 edition.

Publications: *Laudamus*, 1970 and 1984   (See Appendix 1)
                   Selected Slovak Hymns, 1975   (See Appendix 1)

59   GLORY BE TO YOU, O FATHER   8.7.8.7.7.7.8.8.

Based on	Psalm 145:15, 16; Matthew 6:9-13
Theme	Mealtime/Lord's Prayer
Written	22 November 1972
Translation of	*Sláva buď Tobe, Bože náš*, Old Czech Lutheran, 16th cent.
Suggested tune	*FREU DICH SEHR* or *PSALM 42*, Goudimel, 1565

It was customary in Old World families and at church gatherings to sing
a mealtime prayer, and this particular hymn was a standard one. As
Speise Vater, deine Kinder became a favorite table prayer in German
circles, this one served the same function in Slovak homes and churches. I
remember hearing this particular hymn sung at a dinner table in a parsonage in Slovakia within the past decade. The text originated among
Old Czech Lutherans in the 16th century and appeared in the *Cithara
Sanctorum* of 1636. It is usually sung to *FREU DICH SEHR* or to
Goudimel's *PSALM 42*.

60 GOD, MY LORD, MY STRENGTH   10.4.7.5.6.5.

Based on   Psalms 71; 141
Theme   Trust/Cross and Comfort
Written   20 April 1967
Translation of   *Pán Bůh jest má sila*, Old Czech Lutheran, 16th cent.
Suggested tune   *PÁN BŮH*, Prague Gradual, 1576

This translation is a cento and paraphrase of the original six-stanza post-Reformation Old Czech Lutheran hymn as found in the classic Slovak Lutheran hymnal, the *Cithara Sanctorum* of 1636. Taking the thoughts of the original, I restated them in my own style within the metric and melodic parameters of this strong Czech text and tune. The ready adoption of the translation by American congregations testifies to the hymn's adaptability while providing the church with a sturdy affirmation of trust and a melody that conveys the strength of the text.

Publications: (See Appendix 1)
                  Worship Supplement, 1969
                  Selected Slovak Hymns, 1875
                  Lutheran Book of Worship, 1978

61 GREET NOW THE SWIFTLY CHANGING YEAR   LM (8.8.8.8.)

Based on   Psalm 90; Luke 2:21
Theme   New Year's Day/Name of Jesus
Written   14 January 1968
Translation of   *Rok nový zase k nám prišel*, Old Czech Lutheran,
                  17th cent.
Suggested tune   *ROK NOVÝ*, Závorka's *Kancionál, 1602*

Perhaps the most traditional New Year's and Name of Jesus hymn in Slovak hymnody is this 16th-century Old Czech Lutheran favorite. My earliest memory of it goes back to my childhood years in East Chicago, Indiana, and the observance of New Year's Eve in our parsonage, when we would gather around my mother at the piano at midnight and sing this ancient hymn. The next morning the walls of the church next door shook to the exuberant singing of it by the congregation. My translation reduces the original 15 stanzas to seven. The first line of the English text has undergone several changes, the first of which reacted to the inclusive language movement which asserted itself shortly after the hymn was translated, beginning "Greet, man, the swiftly . . ." This was altered to

"Now greet . . ." and finally, to "Greet now . . ." which I prefer. It may be found under any of the three opening lines.

The traditional tune, here taking its title from the opening words of the original text, *ROK NOVÝ* (New Year), is from Závorka's *Kancionál,* 1602. The tune appears in both isometric and rhythmic forms, the latter being the older and preferred by the latest tune book. As a curiosity that may interest someone other than myself, while recuperating after an operation in the hospital on Christmas Eve, 1983, I heard a recording of a Corelli *Concerto Grosso*, one of whose themes closely resembled this old hymn tune.

Publications: (See Appendix 1)
                   Worship Supplement, 1969
                   Selected Slovak Hymns, 1975
                   Lutheran Book of Worship, 1978
                   Lutheran Worship, 1982
                   The Summit Choirbook, 1983
                   The Hymnal 1982, 1985
                   Greet Now the Swiftly Changing Year, 1985
                      (See Appendix 3-A)

62   HEAR ME, O MY PRECIOUS LOVE   Irregular

Based on   2 Corinthians 1:2-7
Theme   Lent/Repentance
Written   27 November 1939, rev. 8 May 1967
Translation of *O lásko má, uslyš mne*, by Jeremiáš Lednický (d. 1685)
Suggested tune *O LÁSKO MÁ*, P. Fábry ms. 1698

This Lenten hymn, bearing the Latin subtitle, *Amor meus, audi me*, was either written by Jeremiás Lednický (d. 1685), or was a translation of a Latin hymn or ode by that title. Lednický was the Slovak Lutheran author of 25 hymns, 14 of them original. This typically Pietistic hymn was a Lenten favorite in my father's church, and one I enjoyed accompanying the congregation on the organ during Lenten vespers in my late teens. It was my first attempt at hymn translation at the age of twenty in East Chicago, Indiana, while I was working nights at the Inland Steel mill, earning tuition for my seminary education.

63 HOW LOVELY AND HOW PLEASANT   7.6.7.6.7.6.

Based on   Psalm 133
Theme   Unity/Harmony
Written   18 March 1966
Translation of   *Jak rozkošne a skvele*, author unknown
Suggested tune   *WIR HATTEN GEBAUET*, German folk tune, 1823

This Slovak text is evidently a versification of Psalm 133, but the original
has been either lost or misplaced. At any rate, it antedated and indirectly
inspired the original hymn. I wrote five years later, "How pleasant, Lord,
when people live." The tune for this hymn likewise cannot be recalled,
though it can be sung nicely to the German folk tune, *WIR HATTEN
GEBAUET*, a Christmas melody for "When Christmas morn is
dawning."

64 LET OUR GLADNESS BANISH SADNESS   14.14.6.6.14.

Based on   Luke 2:1-14
Theme   Christmas/Incarnation
Written   21 November 1957
Translation of   *Čas radosti*, Slovak version of *Omnis mundus jucundetur*
                  by unknown author, 17th cent.
Suggested tune   *ČAS RADOSTI*, 14th cent. Bohemian melody

Not strictly a carol, this Christmas hymn deserves special mention. It is
the *Adeste fideles* of Slovak Christians, whether Lutheran or Catholic. It
is probably of medieval Latin origin, identified as *Omnis mundus jucundetur*, and may go back as far as the 14th century with its Latin text and
Bohemian tune. The Slovak version appeared in *Cantus Catholici* in 1655,
from which it moved into the later editions of the Lutheran *Cithara Sanctorum*, and from thence into two English versions, as "Come rejoicing,
praises voicing" in the *Lutheran Hymnal*, 1941, in a composite translation,
and then in the *Lutheran Book of Worship*, 1978, in a conflation incorpo-
rating most of my translation. This version appears without alteration in
a number of Slovak carol collections and choir settings.

Publications: *Slovak Christmas Carols*, 1957   (See Appendix 2)
                  12 Slovak Carols, 1958   (See Appendix 2)
                  Slovak Christmas, 1960   (See Appendix 2)
                  Slovak Christmas Carols, 1961   (See Appendix 3-B)
                  Selected Slovak Hymns, 1975   (See Appendix 1)
                  Lutheran Book of Worship, 1978   (See Appendix 1)

65 MAKE SONGS OF JOY   8.4.8.4.

Based on	1 Corinthians 15:20-26, 55-57
Theme	Easter
Written	11 March 1976
Translation of	*Zpivejmež všickni vesele*, by Juraj Tranovský 1636
Suggested tune	*ZPIVEJMEŽ VŠICKNI VESELE*, Chorvát *Velká Partitúra*, 1936

Only two Slovak Easter hymns were to be found in the *Lutheran Hymnal* of 1941. The publication of the *Lutheran Book of Worship* (1978) afforded an opportunity to add another translation of a Tranovský hymn dating from 1636, but to a melody of unknown date from the *Velká Partitúra* (Large Tune Book) of Juraj Chorvát (1936). The original 12-stanza text was condensed to six, retaining representative stanzas for use in an era when lengthy hymns are no longer in vogue.

66 YOUR HEART, O GOD, IS GRIEVED   LM (8.8.8.8.) and chant

Based on	Psalm 51
Theme	Kyrie/Repentance
Written	24 September 1969
Translation of	*Známe to, Pane Bože nás*, Juraj Tranovský, 1636
Suggested tune	*ZNÁME TO, PANE BOŽE NÁS*, Škultéty *Partitúra*, 1798

The Slovak Lutheran hymnal, the *Tranoscius*, contains at least 12 Kyries for liturgical use during the church year. One of the general Kyries is this 9-stanza hymn which I abbreviated to three and translated for *Laudamus*, the Lutheran World Federation hymnbook of 1970. Usually each section of the Kyrie is addressed to one of the Persons of the Trinity and is prefaced by a chant sung by the worship leader, or cantor. I retained that distinctive element in this abbreviated version.

I have replaced the word "feeble" in 3:2 with the word "reborn" because "feeble" seemed to imply that the Spirit creates a weak person rather than a new person who is born small and weak and grows stronger as one matures.

This type of Kyrie can be substituted for the liturgical responses if Luther's *Deutsche Messe* is used.

Publications: *Laudamus*, 1970   (See Appendix 1)
                  Selected Slovak Hymns, 1975   (See Appendix 1)
                  Lutheran Book of Worship, 1978   (See Appendix 1)
                  Laudamus, 1984   (See Appendix 1)
                  Hymnal Supplement II, 1987   (See Appendix 1)

67   A CUCKOO FLEW OUT OF THE WOOD   12.12.9.9.12.

Theme   Christmas
Translated   1965
Translation of   *Hla, kukučka nechala les* (Slovak carol, origin unknown)

Publications: *Christmas*, 1967   (See Appendix 2)
                  [The version in *Christmas*, 1967 is one syllable
                  short in lines 3 and 4 in stanzas 2 and 3.]

68   CHRISTIANS, GATHER ROUND   5.5.5.5.8.8.5.5.

Theme   Christmas Eve
Translated   1957
Translation of   *Dobrá novina* (Andrej Ozym, *Kancionál*, Turčiansky
                  Sv. Martin, Czechoslovakia, 1805)

Publications: *Slovak Christmas*, 1960   (See Appendix 2)
                  Slovak Christmas Carols, 1961   (See Appendix 3-B)
                  Four Slovak Carols, 1976   (See Appendix 3-B)

69   COME NOW, SHEPHERDS, QUICKLY COME   14.14.8.8.6.5.

Theme   Christmas Eve
Translated   1957
Translation of   *Pospešte sem, pastuškovia* (Vojtech Wick in *Nebeské
                  Hlasy*, Košice, Czechoslovakia, 1924)

Publications: *12 Slovak Carols*, 1958   (See Appendix 2)
                  Slovak Christmas, 1960   (See Appendix 2)
                  Slovak Christmas Carols, 1961   (See Appendix 3-B)
                  Make We Joy Now in This Fest, 1971 (XI)
                       (See Appendix 3-B)

70   DEAR LITTLE JESUS, WE COME TO THY BED   10.10.5.5.9.9.10.

Theme	Christmas
Translated	1957
Translation of	*Prišli sme ku tebe, Jezuliatko* (Štefan Pyšný, Ms. collection in Archives of the Society of St. Adalbert, Trnava, Czechoslovakia, 1932)

Publications: *Slovak Christmas Carols*, 1957   (See Appendix 2)
                 12 Slovak Carols, 1958   (See Appendix 2)
                 Slovak Christmas, 1960   (See Appendix 2)
                 Slovak Christmas Carols, 1961   (See Appendix 3-B)
                 Christmas, 1964   (See Appendix 1)

71   HEAVEN'S DAWN IS BREAKING BRIGHTLY   13.13.5.5.13.13.

Theme	Christmas
Translated	1957
Translation of	*Svetlo svetu dnes nastalo* (Text by Andrej Hlinka, tune by Jozef Chládek, in *Nábožný kresťan*, Ruzomberok, Czechoslovakia, 1928)

Publications: *Slovak Christmas Carols*, 1957   (See Appendix 2)
                 12 Slovak Carols, 1958   (See Appendix 2)
                 Slovak Christmas, 1960   (See Appendix 2)
                 Slovak Christmas Carols, 1961   (See Appendix 3-B)
                 Four Slovak Carols, 1976   (See Appendix 3-B)

72   LO, OUR SHEPHERD IN A MANGER   8.8.7.11.

Theme	Christmas
Translated	1957
Translation of	*Dobrý pastier sa narodil* (Text by Andrej Hlinka (1864-1938, tune by Josef Chládek *(1836-1928) in Nábožný krestan*, Ruzomberok, Czechoslovakia, 1928)

Publications: *Slovak Christmas*, 1960   (See Appendix 2)

73 LO, WHAT A WONDER   11.11.10.10.

Theme   Christmas
Translated   1957
Translation of   *Veselosť velká sa svetu zjavila* (Text by Andrej Hlinka
                 in *Nábožný krestan*, Ružomberok, Czechoslovakia,
                 1921; tune origin unknown)

Publications: *12 Slovak Carols*, 1958   (See Appendix 2)
                 Slovak Christmas Carols, 1961   (See Appendix 3-B)

74 OH, WHAT TIDINGS BRIGHT   10.10.8.8.10.

Theme   Christmas Eve
Translated   1979
Translation of   *Dobrá novina* (See notes on earlier translation of this
                 carol under title of CHRISTIANS, GATHER
                 ROUND.)

Publications: *Oh, What Tidings Bright*, 1980   (See Appendix 3-B)

75 OUT OF THE FOREST A CUCKOO FLEW   11.11.9.9.(8).6.

Theme   Christmas
Translated   1965
Translation of   *Zezulka z lesa vylitla* (Czech carol of unknown origin)

Publications: *Christmas*, 1967   (See Appendix 1)

76 OUT TO THE HILLS   9.9.8.8.9.9.

Theme   Christmas Eve
Translated   1957
Translation of   *Do hory, do lesa, valasi* (Text by Andrej Hlinka, tune
                 by Jozef Chladek, in *Nábožný krestan*, Ružomberok,
                 Czechoslovakia, 1928)

Publications: *12 Slovak Carols*, 1958   (See Appendix 2)
                 Slovak Christmas, 1960   (See Appendix 2)
                 Slovak Christmas Carols, 1961   (See Appendix 3-B)

77   RISE UP, BETHL'EM SHEPHERDS, RISE   7.7.5.5.8.8.5.5.

Theme	Christmas Eve
Translated	1957
Translation of	*Vstante hore, valasi* (Štefan Pyšný ms. collection in Archives of the Society of St. Adalbert, Trnava, Czechoslovakia, 1932)
Publications:	*12 Slovak Carols*, 1958 (See Appendix 2)
	Slovak Christmas, 1960 (See Appendix 2)
	Slovak Christmas Carols, 1961 (See Appendix 3-B)
	Three Slovak Carols, 1980 (See Appendix 3-B)

78   SHEPHERDS ALL, COME   10.10.10.10.4.(10)

Theme	Christmas Eve
Translated	1979
Translation of	*Nesiem vám noviny* (Author and composer unknown, from *Duchovný spevník*, Czechoslovakia, 1882)
Publications:	*Shepherds All, Come*, 1980 (See Appendix 3-B)

79   SHEPHERDS OF BETHLEHEM   6.6.9.6.6.9.5.5.10.10.

Theme	Christmas Eve
Translated	1957
Translation of	*Povstáňte v rýchlosti* (Pavlin Bajan ms. collection, Archives of the Society of St. Adalbert, Trnava, Czechoslovakia, 1783)
Publications:	*Slovak Christmas Carols*, 1957 (See Appendix 2)
	12 Slovak Carols, 1958 (See Appendix 2)
	Slovak Christmas, 1960 (See Appendix 2)
	Slovak Christmas Carols, 1961 (See Appendix 3-B)
	Four Slovak Carols, 1976 (See Appendix 3-B)

80 SLUMBER, LOVELY BABY   6.6.7.7.7.7.6.6.5.5.

Theme	Christmas Eve
Translated	1979, by Andrew Roy and Jaroslav Vajda
Translation of	*Búvaj, dieťa krásne* (Štefan Pyšný, ms. with notes, Vrbov, Czechoslovakia, 1922)

Publications: *Slumber, Lovely Baby*, 1980   (See Appendix 3-B)

81 TELL US, SHEPHERDS, WHY SO JOYFUL   13.13.6.6.7.

Theme	Christmas Eve
Translated	1957
Translation of	*Povedzte nám, pastierovia* (Andrej Ozym *Kancionál*, Archives of the Slovak National Museum, Turc. Sv. Martin, Czechoslovakia, 1808)

Publications: *Slovak Christmas Carols*, 1957   (See Appendix 2)
12 Slovak Carols, 1958   (See Appendix 2)
Slovak Christmas, 1960   (See Appendix 2)
Slovak Christmas Carols, 1961   (See Appendix 3-B)
Make We Joy Now in This Fest, 1971 (XII)
    (See Appendix 3-B)
Four Slovak Carols, 1976   (See Appendix 3-B)

82 WAKE TO THE WONDER   10.10.12.12.10.10.

Theme	Christmas Eve
Translated	1979
Translation of	*Vstávajte, pastieri* (Eastern Slovakia carol, A. Furdanič ms. collection, Archives of the Society of St. Adalbert, Trnava, Czechoslovakia, 1922)

Publications: *Wake to the Wonder*, 1980   (See Appendix 3-B)

83 WAKE UP, BROTHER, LISTEN   11.11.8.11.11.

Theme	Christmas Eve
Translated	1957
Translation of	*Vstávaj, bratku* (origin unknown)

Publications: *12 Slovak Carols*, 1958   (See Appendix 2)

84 WHILE MARY ROCKS HER CHILD TO REST   8.8.8.8.10.10.

Theme   Christmas Eve
Translated   1957
Translation of   *Ked' Mária plačúcemu* (Origin unknown, in *Cantus Catholici* Trnava, Czechoslovakia, 1655)

Publications: *Slovak Christmas Carols*, Duris, 1957
                    (See Appendix 2)
                 12 Slovak Carols, 1958   (See Appendix 2)
                 Slovak Christmas, 1960   (See Appendix 2)
                 Slovak Christmas Carols, 1961   (See Appendix 3-B)
                 Three Slovak Carols, 1976   (See Appendix 3-B)

85 ALL WHO CRAVE A GREATER MEASURE   8.8.8.8.8.8.7.8.8.11.

Theme   Christmas Eve
Translated   4 September 1976
Translation of   *Alle, die ihr Gott zu ehren*, by Paul Gerhardt

Publications: *Be Glad and Sing*, 1976   (See Appendix 2)

86 BREAK FORTH IN PRAISE TO GOD   6.6.6.6.6.7.6.7.6.6.
                                      Refrain

Theme   Trinity/Thanksgiving
Translated   28 October 1979
Translation of   *Auf, auf, du Gottes Lob* by Wilhelm Osterwald (1820-1887)

This hymn to the Holy Trinity as well as the Hymn of the Day for the 15th Sunday after Pentecost (traditional lectionary) was requested by Concordia Publishing House for its choral setting of the German original.

Publications: *Church Choir Book II*, 1981   (See Appendix 2)

87   DEAREST LORD JESUS   Irregular

Theme	Cross and Comfort
Translated	26 November 1986
Translation of	*Liebster Herr Jesu, wo bleibst du so lange*, origin unknown

Publications: *Dearest Lord Jesus*, 1987   (See Appendix 3-B)

88   FOR YOUR MERCY I IMPLORE YOU   8.7.8.7.D.

Theme	Trust
Translated	24 May 1983
Translation of	*Deines Kinds Gebet erhöre*

89   HEAR ME, HELP ME, GRACIOUS SAVIOR   8.7.8.7.

Theme	Cross and Comfort
Translated	10 March 1983
Translation of	*Lass, o Herr, mich Hülfe finden*

90   IF GOD IS ABSENT, ALL THE COST   LM (8.8.8.8.)

Theme	Home/Family
Translated	7 December 1975
Translation of	*Wo Gott zum Haus nicht gibt sein Gunst*, by Johann Kohlross (d. 1558). First stanza: Isaac Watts altered.

91   LORD, WE HOLD YOUR GOODNESS PRECIOUS   8.7.8.7.

Theme	Praise
Translated	13 May 1983
Translation of	*Herr, wir trau'n auf deine Güte*

92   NOW SHINE, BRIGHT GLOW OF MAJESTY   Irregular

Theme   Epiphany
Translated   14 September 1981
Translation of   *Nun schein, du Glanz der Herrlichkeit*, Anon. c. 1590

Publications: Musical setting by Leonard Lechner, Bärenreiter Verlag,
                   Kassel, Germany, 1974

93   O FATHER, SEND THE SPIRIT DOWN   8.8.7.8.8.7.

Theme   Pentecost/Holy Spirit
Translated   23 September 1975
Translation of   *Gott Vater, sende deinen Geist*, stanzas 1 and 2 of a
                   12-stanza hymn by Paul Gerhardt (1656)

94   O JOYOUS CHRISTMAS NIGHT   6.7.6.7.6.6.6.6.

Theme   Christmas Eve
Translated   3 February 1980
Translation of   *Erfreute Weinachtsnacht*, Anon.

Publications: *Christmas Cantata*, 1980   (See Appendix 2)

95   THE RESCUE WE WERE WAITING FOR   8.8.8.8.D.

Theme   Justification
Paraphrased   26 September 1975
Paraphrase of   *Es ist das Heil*, by Paul Speratus, 1523

So many chorales are versified dogma, stating incontrovertible truths in
square solid verse not intended to be judged as poetry, thus resulting in
a boring exercise for many worshipers, especially those for whom the
chorale is strange. I had wondered how certain rugged chorales could be
rewritten in contemporary, more poetic language and illustrated with
more imagery. This paraphrase of *Es ist das Heil* attempts to do that,
and, to the extent that it succeeds, may inspire other experiments that
would retain the strength and certitude of the chorale and garb it in fresh
clothing and personalize the worshiper's response to the faith once
delivered to the saints. I can imagine such confessional (not penitential)

renditions utilizing the pictures and logic of a C. S. Lewis or a Helmut Thielecke to convey the orthodox doctrines in the fresh idiom of today's theologians.

This particular cento (the original had 14 stanzas) and paraphrase has been widely used by individual congregations, but it is not yet known in most Lutheran churches where the 10-stanza translation of the original would be most familiar.

A slight variation in the meter was made in the first and third lines of each stanza, providing a syllable for each note of the line-ending slur, thus propelling the hymn from the very beginning.

96   WHAT LOVE, LORD JESUS, THAT YOU GO   8.7.8.7.4.4.7.4.4.7.

Based on	John 19:16, 17
Theme	Lent
Written	20 July 1987
Suggested tune	*SO GEHST DU NUN*

The English translation of *So gehst du nun, mein Jesu, hin* by Kaspar F. Nachtenhöfer (1651) was made for *The Lutheran Hymnal* (1941) by W. G. Polack. Upon a request from Morning Star Music Publishers, this text was updated and paraphrased for a choral setting of stanzas 1, 3, and 5.

Publications:	*What Love, Lord Jesus, That You Go*, 1988
	(See Appendix 3-B)

97   WORLD, FOR ALL YOUR GAIN
AND PLEASURE   8.7.8.7.7.7.7.7.

Theme	Heaven/Hope
Translated	1 September 1971
Translation of	*Welt, ade, ich bin dein müde*, by Abraham Teller (1649), st. 1, and Johann Georg Albinus (1624-1679), st. 2.
Publications:	*Let All Together Praise*, 1983 (See Appendix 2)

98 A DOVE FLEW DOWN FROM HEAVEN   7.5.7.6.5.5.6.6.6.

Theme   Christmas/Annunciation
Translation   14 October 1970
Translation of   *Es flog ein Täublein weisse*, ca. 1600

Publications: *A Dove Flew Down from Heaven*, 1971
                 (See Appendix 3-B)

99 DELICATE CHILD OF ROYAL LINE   8.7.8.7.4.4.7.

Theme   Christmas Eve
Translated   23 October 1972
Translation of   *Kindelein zart*, Anon.

Publications: *Delicate Child of Royal Line*, 1973
                 (See Appendix 3-B)

100 IN BETHLEHEM A WONDER   7.6.7.6.10.

Theme   Christmas
Translated   1969
Translation of   *Zu Bethlehem geboren*, Frederick von Spee, *Kölner
                 Psalter*, 1638

Publications: *In Bethlehem a Wonder*, 1971   (See Appendix 3-B)

101 NOW TO THIS BABE SO TENDER   7.7.7.7.7.8.5.

Theme   Christmas Eve
Translated   23 October 1972
Translation of   *Lasst uns das Kindlein wiegen*, Anon., 1604

Publications: *Now to this Babe so Tender*, 1973
                 (See Appendix 3-B)

102   SLEEP SOFTLY, SOFTLY, BEAUTIFUL JESUS   10.6.8.8.6.6.

Theme	Christmas Eve
Translated	23 October 1972
Translation of	*O schlafe, lieblicher Jesu*, Anon.

Publications: *Sleep Softly, Softly, Beautiful Jesus*, 1973
                              (See Appendix 2)

103   SLEEP WELL, DEAR HEAVENLY BOY   8.6.8.6.8.8.4.6.

Theme	Christmas Eve
Translated	25 January 1971
Translation of	*Schlaf wohl, du Himmelsknabe du*, Anon., ca. 1850

Publications: *Sleep Well, Dear Heavenly Boy*, 1971
                              (See Appendix 3-B)

104   UP, O SHEPHERDS   7.6.7.6.7.7.7.7.

Theme	Christmas Eve
Translated	25 January 1971, rev. 26 October 1986
Translation of	*Auf, ihr Hirten*, Tyrolean carol

Publications: *Up, O Shepherds*, 1971   (See Appendix 3-B)

105   WAKE, SHEPHERDS, AWAKE   5.5.6.6.5.5.

Theme	Christmas Eve
Translated	23 October 1972
Translation of	*Ihr Hirten, erwacht*, Rhine carol, ca. 1840

Publications: *Wake, Shepherds, Awake*, 1973   (See Appendix 3-B)

106 BLESSED BE THE PRECIOUS BABY LM (8.8.8.8.) Trochaic

Theme	Christmas Eve
Translated	23 March 1983
Translation of	*Adlott légy kisdedecske*, Zoltan Kodály (1882-1967)

This and the following two Hungarian hymns were selected for inclusion in the Lutheran World Federation hymn book, *Laudamus*, for its 1984 meeting in Budapest, Hungary. I was asked to versify the literal English translation.

Publications: *Laudamus*, 1984 (See Appendix 1)

107 FROM THE SHADOW OF MY PAIN 7.7.7.5.5.8.7.

Theme:	Christian Life/Repentance
Translated	23 March 1983
Translation of	*Kinok arnyekaibol*, Weores Sandor (b. 1913)

Publications: *Laudamus*, 1984 (See Appendix 1)

108 WHO'S THAT SITTING ON THE GROUND 7.7.8.5.

Theme	Children
Translated	23 March 1983
Translation of	*Pazzitdombon uldogel*, Szedo Denes (b. 1922)

Publications: *Laudamus*, 1984 (See Appendix 1)

APPENDICES & INDICES

Appendix 1: Hymnals
Listed by year of publication

Worship Supplement, Concordia Publishing House, St. Louis, MO 1969
Contemporary Worship: Hymns, Inter-Lutheran Commission on Worship, 1969

Johannine Hymnal, American Catholic Press, Oak Park, IL 1970
Laudamus (4th ed.), Lutheran World Federation, Geneva, Switzerland 1970
Contemporary Worship: Hymns for Baptism and Communion, ILCW, 1972

The Hymnal of the United Church of Christ, United Church Press, Philadelphia 1974

Worship II (Roman Catholic), GIA Publications, Chicago 1975
Selected Slovak Hymns, Slovak Zion Synod, Lutheran Church in America, Riverside, IL 1975

Ecumenical Praise, Agape (Hope Publishing Company), Carol Stream, IL 1977

Lutheran Book of Worship, (ILCW), Augsburg Publishing House, Minneapolis, MN 1978

Hymns in Large Print (from the LBW), Augsburg Publishing House, Minneapolis, MN 1978

Three Hymns for 1979, The Hymn Society of America, Wittenberg University, Springfield, OH 1979

Choirbook for Saints and Sinners, Agape (Hope Publishing Company), Carol Stream, IL 1980

Catholic Book of Worship II (Choir ed.) Canadian Conference of Catholic Bishops and Gordon V. Thompson, Ltd., Ottawa/Toronto, Canada 1980
Welshire Hymns, Welshire Presbyterian Church, Denver, CO 1980
Hymnal Supplement, Agape (Hope Publishing Company), Carol Stream, IL 1984

Lutheran Worship (Commission on Worship, The Lutheran Church— Missouri Synod) Concordia Publishing House, St. Louis, MO 1982
The Summit Choirbook, The Dominican Nuns of Summit, NJ 1983
Laudamus (5th ed.), Lutheran World Federation, Geneva, Switzerland 1984
The Hymnal 1982 (Episcopal), The Church Hymnal Corporation, New York 1985

Worship (A hymnal and service book for Roman Catholics, 3rd ed.), GIA Publications, Chicago, IL 1986
Psalter Hymnal, The Christian Reformed Church, Grand Rapids, MI 1987
Hymnal Supplement II, Hope Publishing Company, Carol Stream, IL 1987
Songs for a Gospel People, United Church of Canada, Vancouver, BC 1987
Songs of Praise 3, Oxford University Press, London W1, England, 1987

Appendix 2: Collections

Listed by year of publication

Slovak Christmas Carols, compiled by Joseph Duris, Slovak Institute, Cleveland, OH 44104, 1957

12 Slovak Carols, Slovak Institute (see above), 1958

Slovak Christmas, A symposium of songs, customs, and plays, Slovak Institute, Cleveland, OH, and Rome, Italy, 1960

Christmas, An annual of Christmas literature and art, Augsburg Publishing House, Minneapolis, MN 55415, 1964, 1967, 1981, 1987

Make We Joy Now in This Fest, arr. by Carl Schalk, Concordia Publishing House, St. Louis, MO 63118, 1971

Be Glad and Sing, ed. by Paul Thomas, Concordia (see above), 1976

Christmas Cantata, by Johann Samuel Beyer, for SATB, solo voices and instruments, Concordia (see above), 1980 (Ref. Full score: 97-5543, Choir score: 98-2457)

Church Choir Book II, ed. by Paul Thomas, for SATB, Concordia (see above), 1981 (Ref. 97-5610)

Let All Together Praise, ed. by Paul Thomas for SATB and instruments, Concordia (see above), 1983 (Ref. Choir: 97-5658, Instr. 97-5659)

Eight Psalms, choral anthem ed. by Carl Schalk, text by Jaroslav Vajda, SATB w/opt. keyboard or cello, Augsburg (see above), 1987

Appendix 3: Sheet Music

Listed alphabetically

A. ORIGINAL TEXTS

Amid the world's bleak wilderness
set to a tune by Richard Hillert for SATB and organ, Ausburg Publishing House, Minneapolis, MN, 55415, 1980 (Ref. 11-1997)

Before the marvel of this night
set to a tune by Carl Schalk for SATB and organ, Augsburg (see above), 1982 (Ref. 11-2005)

Come, Lord Jesus
set to a tune by Donald Busarow for vocal solo and organ, Concordia Publishing House, St. Louis, MO 63118, 1980 (Ref. High voice: 97-5590 and 97-5576, Low voice: 97-5591 and 97-5577)

Gather your children, dear Savior, in peace
set to *SLANE* by Carl Schalk for SATB and organ, Morning Star Music Publishers, St. Louis, MO 63118-4310, 1987 (Ref. MSM 50-8500)

set to a tune by Allan Mahnke for SATB and organ, Concordia (see above), 1987 (Ref. 98-2793)

Go, my children, with my blessing
set to *AR HYD Y NOS*, arr. by Carl Schalk for SATB and organ, as alternate text to "God who made the earth and heaven" under that title, Concordia (see above), 1984 (Ref. 98-2674)

set to *AR HYD Y NOS*, arr. by Walter Pelz for SATB and organ, Morning Star (see above), 1987 (Ref. MSM-50-8900)

Greet now the swiftly changing year
setting by Alfred Fedak for SATB and organ, Concordia (see above), 1985 (Ref. 98-2691)

Now at the peak of wonder
setting by Richard W. Gieseke, concertato for congregation, SAB, organ, brass quartet and timpani, GIA Publications, Chicago, IL 60638, 1983 (Ref. G-2675)

Now the silence
set to *NOW*, tune and arr. by Carl Schalk for SATB, Agape, Carol Stream, IL 60188, 1986 (Ref. AG 72-78)

set to *NOW*, tune by Carl Schalk, arr. for handbells by Cathy Mocklebust, Agape (see above), 1987 (Ref. 1283)

Readings from Acts, versified

texts in *Easter Motets* by Christopher Tye, ed. by Carl Schalk for SATB, Augsburg (see above), Series A, 1986 (11-5749), Series B, 1984 (11-5750), Series C, 1985 (11-5751)

See this wonder in the making

set to *TRYGGARE KAN INGEN VARA*, arr. by Carl Schalk, Morning Star (see above), 1988

This love

set to a tune by Donald Busarow for vocal solo and organ, Concordia (see above), 1980 (Ref. High voice: 97-5588 and 97-5576, Low voice: 97-5589 and 97-5577)

There through endless ranks of angels

tune and setting by Carl Schalk for SATB and organ, Augsburg (see above), 1974 (Ref. 11-1742)

This touch of love

set to a tune by Carl Schalk for congregation, SATB, and organ, Morning Star (see above), 1988 (Ref. MSM-50-8301)

Up through endless ranks of angels

set to *ASCENDED TRIUMPH*, arr. by Walter L. Pelz for SATB and organ, Concordia (see above), 1976 (Ref. 98-2324)

set to *ASCENDED TRIUMPH*, setting and concertato arr. by Henry V. Gerike for congregation, SAB, trumpet and organ, Concordia (see above), 1986 (Ref. 98-2709)

Where shepherds lately knelt

tune and setting by Carl Schalk, arr. for SATB and organ, Augsburg (see above), 1987

B. TRANSLATIONS

A dove flew down from heaven

tr. of *Es flog ein Täublein weisse*, setting by Hermann Schroeder for SATB violins and flute, or organ, Concordia (see above), 1971 (Ref. 98-2061)

Dearest Lord Jesus, why are you delaying

tr. of *Liebster Herr Jesu, wo bleibst du so lange*, Advent anthem by Dietrich Buxtehude, arr. and ed. by Richard Peck for SSATB, Morning Star (see above), 1987 (Ref. MSM-70-1)

Delicate Child of royal line

tr. of *Kindelein zart*, setting by Hermann Schroeder for SATB, 2 flutes and bassoon or 2 violins and cello, or organ, or a cappella, Concordia (see above), 1973 (Ref. 98-2071)

Four Slovak Carols

arr. by Carl Schalk for SATB, Concordia (see above), 1976 (Ref. 98-2271)

In Bethlehem a wonder

tr. of *Zu Bethlehem geboren*, setting by Hermann Schroeder for SATB and flute, violin or oboe, Concordia (see above), 1971 (Ref. 98-2063)

Now to this Babe so tender

tr. of *Lasst uns das Kindlein wiegen*, setting by Hermann Schroeder for flute and violin, or organ, Concordia (see above), 1973 (Ref. 98-2070)

Oh, what tidings bright

tr. of *Dobrá novina*, arr. by Alexander Moyzes for SSATBB, Concordia (see above), 1980 (Ref. 92-2460)

Shepherds all, come

tr. of *Nesiem vám noviny*, arr. by Alexander Moyzes for SSATBB, Concordia (see above), 1980 (Ref. 98-2463)

Sleep softly, beautiful Jesus

tr. of *O schlafe, lieblicher Jesu*, setting by Hermann Schroeder for SATB, violin or oboe, cello or bassoon, or organ, or a cappella, Concordia (see above), 1973 (Ref. 98-2069)

Sleep well, dear heavenly Boy

tr. of *Schlaf wohl, du Himmelsknabe du*, setting by Hermann Schroeder for SATB, 2 flutes and cello, or organ, Concordia (see above), 1971 (Ref. 98-2067)

Slovak Christmas Carols

arr. for SATB, SAB, TTBB, World Library of Sacred Music, Cincinnati, OH 45214, 1961

Slumber, lovely Baby

tr. of *Búvaj, dieta krásne*, arr. by Alexander Moyzes for SSATBB, Concordia (see above), 1980 (Ref. 98-2462)

Three Slovak Carols

arr. by Carl Schalk for SATB, Concordia (see above), 1976 (Ref. 98-2467)

Up, O shepherds

tr. of *Auf, ihr Hirten*, setting by Hermann Schroeder for SAT, flute and violin, or organ, Concordia (see above), 1971 (Ref. 98-2066)

Wake, shepherds, awake

tr. of *Ihr Hirten, erwacht*, setting by Hermann Schroeder for SAT, flute and 2 violins, or organ, Concordia (see above), 1973 (Ref. 98-2068)

Wake to the wonder

tr. of *Vstávajte, pastieri*, arr. by Alexander Moyzes for SSATBB, Concordia (see above), 1980 (Ref. 98-2461)

What love, Lord Jesus, that you go

revised tr. of *So gehst du nun, mein Jesu, hin*, setting by Charles Schramm, Jr. for SAB, Morning Star (see above), 1988 (Ref. MSM-50-3401)

Subject Index

Translated texts: (S) = Slovak, (G) = German, (H) = Hungarian, (C) = Czech

THE CHURCH YEAR

Advent
Gift of joy

Christmas (See also Christmas Carols)
Before the marvel of this night
Gift of joy
Let our gladness banish sadness (S)
Peace came to earth
Rock-a-bye, my dear little Boy
Where shepherds lately knelt

New Year
Greet now the swiftly changing year (S)

Epiphany
Now shine, bright glow of majesty (G)

Lent
Hear me, O my precious love (S)
What love, Lord Jesus, that you go (G)
Your heart, O God, is grieved (S)

Easter
Begin the song of glory now
Make songs of joy (S)

Easter Cycle
Readings from Acts, versified

Easter V
Amid the world's bleak wilderness

Ascension
Ascending, Christ returns to God (S)
Up through endless ranks of angels

Pentecost
O Father, send the Spirit down (G)

Trinity
Break forth in praise to God (G)
O God, eternal Father

THE CHURCH

Children
Someone special
Who's that sitting on the ground (H)

Commemorations
A comet blazed across the skies (Luther's birthday)
Far from the time when we were few (Church in a new land)
God who built this wondrous planet (Church dedication)
Here is the living proof, good Lord (Mortgage-burning)
Let us praise our gracious God (Anniversary of immigration)
Now, at the peak of wonder (Church anniversary)
Pass in review (Ministerial anniversary/retirement)
This is a time for banners and bells (Church anniversary)
Who could have dreamt a land like this (National anniversary)
You are the rock (Church anniversary)

Confirmation
O day of days
The friend I need

Family (See The Christian Life)

Heaven/Eternal Life
How meager and mundane
Then the glory
World, for all your gain (G)

House of God
God, who built this wondrous planet
Now the silence

Marriage
Come, Lord Jesus, to this place
This love, O Christ

Mission/Ministry/Witness
Catch the vision! Share the glory!
Far from the time when we were few
Pass in review
You are the King

Peace/Unity
Go, my children, with my blessing
How lovely and how pleasant (S)
How pleasant, Lord, when brothers live
Lord, as you taught us once to pray

Praise (See The Christian Life)
God of the sparrow
Now the silence
Where you are, there is life

Prayer (See The Christian Life)

Repentance/Forgiveness (See The Christian Life)

Service/Social Concern
Creator, keeper, caring Lord (Health and healing)
God of the sparrow
You are the Shepherd (Care of the aged)

Thanksgiving (See Praise)
Count your blessings, O my soul
God of the sparrow

WORSHIP/LITURGY

Entrance
Now the silence

Confession/Kyrie
Your heart, O God, is grieved (S)

Credo
O God, eternal Father, Lord

Psalms
You, Jesus, are my Shepherd true (Ps. 23)
I praise you, Lord, in every hour (Ps. 30)
Though mountains quake (Ps. 46)
O dearest Friend (Ps. 51)
Before your awesome majesty (Ps. 93)
Give glory, all creation (Ps. 103)
Count your blessings, O my soul (Ps. 104)
Lord, I must praise you (Ps. 111)
In hopelessness and near despair (Ps. 130)
How lovely and how pleasant (Ps. 133)

Baptism

Go, my children, with my blessing
See this wonder in the making
This child of ours

Communion

Come in holy awe and truth (S)
Now the silence
This touch of love

Dismissal/Benediction

Go, my children, with my blessing
Then the glory

THE CHRISTIAN LIFE

Children

I have a Father you would like (Witness)
Someone special
Who's that sitting on the ground (H)

Cross and comfort

From the shadow of my pain (H)
Hear me, help me, precious Savior (G)
Hear me, O my precious love (S)

Discipleship

Christ goes before
O day of days, the day I found
Who is this who comes from nowhere

Faith

Amid the world's bleak wilderness
Christ goes before
Who is this who comes from nowhere

Family

Gather your children, dear Savior, in peace
If God is absent (G)

Gratitude

God of the sparrow
Lord, I must praise you

Justification

The rescue we were waiting for (G)

Love

How pleasant, Lord, when brothers live
Lord, as you taught us once to pray
Where you are, there is life

Peace/Unity

How lovely and how pleasant (S)
Where you are, there is life

Praise

Before your awesome majesty
Count your blessings, O my soul
Break forth in praise to God (G)
Give glory, all creation
God of the sparrow
I praise you, Lord, in every hour
Lord, I must praise you

Prayer

Dear Father God, we rise to say (S) (Morning)
Glory be to you, O Father (S)

Repentance/Forgiveness

For your mercy I implore you (G)
Hear me, help me, precious Savior (G)
Hear me, O my precious Love (S)
How could I hurt you so
I praise you, Lord, in every hour
In hopelessness and near despair
O dearest Friend
Your heart, O God, is grieved (S)

Service

God of the sparrow
Creator, Keeper, caring Lord
You are the Shepherd

Trust

God, my Lord, my strength (S)
Lord, I must praise you
Lord, we hold your goodness precious (G)
Though mountains quake and oceans roar
You, Jesus, are my Shepherd true

CHRISTMAS SONGS AND CAROLS

German

A dove flew down from heaven
All who crave a greater measure
Delicate Child of royal line
In Bethlehem, a wonder
Now to the Babe so tender
O joyous Christmas night
Sleep softly, softly, beautiful Jesus
Sleep well, dear heavenly Boy
Up, O shepherds
Wake, shepherds, awake

Slovak

A cuckoo flew out of the wood
Christians, gather round
Come now, shepherds, quickly come
Dear little Jesus, we come to your bed
Heaven's dawn is breaking brightly
Let our gladness banish sadness
Lo, a Shepherd in a manger
Oh, what tidings bright
Out to the hills
Rise up, Bethl'em shepherds, rise
Shepherds all, come
Shepherds of Bethlehem
Slumber, lovely baby
Tell us, shepherds, why so joyful
Wake to the wonder appearing above
Wake up, brothers, listen
While Mary rocks her child to rest

Metrical Index

4.4.8.4.4.4.
This touch of love

4.5.7.4.5.7.
The friend I need

5.4.6.7.7.
God of the sparrow

5.5.5.5.8.8.5.5.
Christians, gather round

5.5.6.6.5.5.
Wake, shepherds, awake

6.6.6.8.8.6.4.
Where you are, there is life

6.6.8.4.4.4.8.
How could I hurt you so
How meager and mundane

6.7.6.7.6.6.6.6.
O joyous Christmas night

7.6.7.6.5.5.6.6.6.
A dove flew down from heaven

7.6.7.6.7.6.
How lovely and how pleasant

7.6.7.6.D.
Christians, let us remember

7.6.7.6.7.7.7.7.
Up, O shepherds

7.6.7.6.10.
In Bethlehem, a wonder

7.7.5.5.8.8.5.5.
Rise up, Bethl'em shepherds

7.7.7.5.5.8.7.
From the shadow of my pain

7.7.7.7.
Come, Lord Jesus, to this place

7.7.7.7. and Alleluias
Let us praise our gracious God

7.7.7.7.5.5.6.
Now, at the peak of wonder

7.7.7.7.7.7.
Someone Special

7.7.7.7.7.7.7.7.
Count your blessings, O my soul

7.7.7.7.7.8.5.
Now to the Babe so tender

7.7.8.5.
Who's that sitting on the ground

7.8.7.8.7.7.
Come in holy awe and truth

8.4.8.4.
Ascending, Christ returns to God
Make songs of joy

8.4.8.4.8.8.8.4.
Go, my children, with my blessing

CM (8.6.8.6.)
Far from the time when we were few
Here is the living proof, good Lord
How pleasant, Lord, when brothers live
I have a father you would like
Readings from Acts, versified
You are the Shepherd

8.6.8.6.8.6.
Creator, Keeper, caring Lord

8.6.8.6.8.8.4.6.
Sleep well, dear heavenly Boy

- 207 -

8.7.8.7.
Hear me, help me, gracious Savior
Lord, we hold your goodness precious

8.7.8.7.4.4.7.
Delicate Child of royal line

8.7.8.7.4.4.7.4.4.7.
What love, Lord Jesus, that you go

8.7.8.7.7.7.7.7.
World, for all your gain

8.7.8.7.7.7.8.8.
Glory be to you, O Father

8.7.8.7.8.7.
God, who built this wondrous planet
Up through endless ranks of angels

8.7.8.7.D.
For your mercy I implore you

8.7.8.7.8.8.7.
In hopelessness and near despair
You are the rock
You, Jesus, are my Shepherd true

8.7.8.7.8.8.8.7.
Who is this who comes from nowhere

8.8.7.11.
Lo, our Shepherd in a manger

8.8.8. and Alleluias
O God, eternal Father, Lord

LM (8.8.8.8.)
A comet blazed across the skies
Before your awesome majesty
Blessed be the precious Baby (trochaic)
Dear Father God, we rise to say
Greet now the swiftly changing year
If God is absent, all the cost
O day of days, the day I found
See this wonder in the making (trochaic)
Your heart, O God, is grieved

LM (8.8.8.8.) and Refrain
This child of ours

8.8.8.8.8.8.8.6.
Before the marvel of this night

LMD (8.8.8.8.D.)
Begin the song of glory now
The rescue we were waiting for

8.8.8.8.10.10.
While Mary rocks her child

9.7.9.7. and Refrain
This is a time for banners and bells

9.9.8.8.9.8.9.
Catch the vision! Share the glory!

9.9.8.8.9.9.
Out to the hills

10.4.7.5.6.5.
God, my Lord, my strength

10.6.8.8.6.6.
Sleep softly, beautiful Jesus

10.8.10.8.10.10.
This love, O Christ

10.10.8.8.10.
Oh, what tidings bright

10.10.10.8.8.
Peace came to earth

10.10.10.10.
Pass in review

10.10.10.10.4.(10)
Shepherds all, come

14 lines of 10'
You are the King

10.10.12.12.10.10.
Wake to the wonder

10.11.11.12.
Gather your children, dear Savior,
    in peace

11.11.8.11.11.
Wake up, brothers

11.11.10.10.
Lo, what a wonder

12.10.8.8.8.10.
Rock-a-bye, my dear little Boy

12.10.12.10.12.10.12.12.
O dearest Friend

12.12.9.9.12.
A cuckoo flew out of the wood

12.12.10.10.
Where shepherds lately knelt

13.13.6.6.7.
Tell us, shepherds, why so joyful

14.14.6.6.14.
Let our gladness banish sadness

14.14.8.8.6.5.
Come now, shepherds, quickly

Irregular

All who crave a greater measure
Amid the world's bleak wilderness
Break forth in praise to God
Christ goes before
Dear little Jesus, we come to your bed
Dearest Lord Jesus, why are you delaying

Gift of joy
Give glory, all creation
Hear me, O my precious Love
Heaven's dawn is breaking brightly
I praise you, Lord, in every hour
Lord, I must praise you
Now shine, bright glow of majesty
Now the silence

Out of the forest a cuckoo flew
Shepherds of Bethlehem
Slumber, lovely Baby
Then the glory
Though mountains quake and oceans roar
Who could have dreamt a land like this

Index of Scripture Texts

Index of First Lines

Translated texts: (S) = Slovak, (G) = German, (H) = Hungarian, (C) = Czech